Leadership Intelligence equips leaders with ideas, s helpful framework, all designed to enab themselves and in others. *Leadership Intelligence* is a gift to all leaders. It is a substantive and inspiring book filled with evidence-based insights that are immediately useful.

—**Jane E. Dutton**, Robert L. Kahn Distinguished University Professor of Business Administration and Psychology, University of Michigan

Leadership Intelligence is a practical book about bringing out the best in others. Using new studies and examples, Gene Harker highlights strategies for enhancing your competence, confidence, energy, attention, and sense of purpose.

—**Adam Grant**, Wharton professor and *New York Times* best-selling author of *Give and Take*

Looking to energize your organization? *Leadership Intelligence* draws together contemporary research from positive psychology into a readable and practical guide for managers who want more engaged employees—and a more vital leadership experience.

—**Richard M. Ryan**, Institute for Positive Psychology and Education, Australian Catholic University

Leadership Intelligence is about more than building a successful you; it's also about building better organizations and communities from which we will all benefit. This book is chock-full of insights and examples for guiding you on your personal journey to a wholehearted, meaningful life. Dr. Gene hits the nail on the head for those leaders, like me, who are ultimately looking to inspire the best from others in order to accomplish great things.

—**Daniel Spillman**, In-house IP Counsel for a Fortune 50 company

Concise, direct, and powerful. With many years of experience in leadership, organizational development, and executive recruiting, I was surprised to find something to strike me with such impact. The competencies that Dr. Harker has identified will enable you to become a leader people want to follow. The self-assessment and applications throughout the book are excellent and will have a lasting impact on your personal and professional pursuits.

—**Jon Sarn**, Executive Vice President, The Kinsey Group

Dr. Harker is right. We are all leaders in various aspects of our lives, no matter what age or stage. How one leads is a decision that the book both challenges and supports through a series of experiments and suggested activities designed to help us reach personal and team potential. While I wish I'd had the opportunity to read this book many years ago, it is clear that I am still in process. For the recent retiree such as myself, the book is loaded with ideas for self-improvement and increasing the quality of personal relationships. I recommend *Leadership Intelligence* for any individual seeking continued personal development.

—**Sara B. Wills, Ph.D.**, Manager Agency Recruiting (retired) for a large U.S. insurance and financial services company

Gene Harker delivers a compelling wake-up call to would-be leaders. *Leadership Intelligence* reinvigorates passion across emotional, physical, and relational ways of being. Before you can lead others to great achievement, you must first sharpen your own LI. Use this book as a practical guide in your journey.

—**James Lee**, CIO and Vice President, Wabash National Corporation

Are you a leader? Are you any good? How would you know? *Leadership Intelligence* unpacks critical elements of successful leadership by revealing why bringing out the best in others begins with bringing out the best in you!

—**W. Graham Carlos, M.D.**, Assistant Professor of Clinical Medicine, Indiana University School of Medicine

What if everyone in your family, on your team, or in your organization knew how to bring out the best in themselves and everyone else in the group? *Leadership Intelligence* is the book that can get you there. Dr. Harker is that rare author who combines solid research with engaging prose and immediately applicable principles. One gets the sense that he's seen firsthand how these six leadership qualities profoundly affect any living environment, and is excited to help his readers do the same. In a world of isolated individuals grasping for personal gain, *Leadership Intelligence* is a game changer.

—**Susan Bondurant**, Registered Nurse, Eskenazi Health

Leadership Intelligence blends the scholarship of a grad-school textbook with practical insights from a real-world leader. This is a must-read for new and experienced leaders alike.

—**Rob Parker**, CEO, Southern Ground & the Zac Brown Band

Dr. Harker brings forth a clear, challenging, and inspirational deep dive into leadership. I strongly suggest that *Leadership Intelligence* becomes a staple on the reading list of all who aspire to be their best. You will enjoy the journey!

—**Ralph Reiff**, Founder and Executive Director, St. Vincent Sports Performance; Manager of Athlete Care for the 1996 Centennial Olympic Games

Dr. Gene Harker has provided a resource that applies theory, common sense, and holistic healthcare with practice he calls experiments. We can do an experiment; we can do an assessment; we can improve our leadership intelligence and impact all those around us toward a more fulfilling life. Who wouldn't want that?

—**Karen J. Diefendorf**, Chaplain, Lt. Col., U.S. Army (retired)

There's a void of true leadership in American society today. *Leadership Intelligence* provides the prescription to fill that void. Gene Harker addresses the practical realities of human behavior and pulls out the keys to successful leadership.

—**Jeff McClintic**, Senior Vice President, hhgregg

Gene Harker's book *Leadership Intelligence* is a unique and intentionally different approach to leadership development, focusing not on bettering oneself, but intentionally trying to better others by helping them realize their full potential. This unique approach to leadership impacts not only a few individuals in a current sphere within a generation, but has the potential to positively impact hundreds of thousands or millions of people in future generations. This is a book I'll be recommending.

—**Bill Dull**, Owner/Director, BriarTek Incorporated

Gene Harker's *Leadership Intelligence* is a smart read! The careful research and intellect of a respected physician is combined with the tact of a trusted advisor to deliver managerial wisdom in an easy-to-consume, easy-to-remember package. Dr. Harker's practical counsel leverages the primary learning styles beginning with verbal instruction, followed by visual representation, leading to kinetic "experiments" that enable the reader to move seamlessly from learning to implementing. Gene guides the leader through personal transformation prior to connecting with his or her team. Although useful for anyone, *Leadership Intelligence* is a must-read for all leaders.

—**Bob Pourcho**, Owner and President, RBP Solutions

Dr. Harker offers an exciting new entry into the market of leadership teaching, taking a refreshing and often-neglected approach by seamlessly combining theoretical concepts with practical applications. His concept of *grit* runs like a thread through the material, tying together the teaching material to the ultimate conclusion, and is backed up by real-life examples. This approach is wrapped up with a fantastic set of assessments to provide real-time feedback to the reader on the application of the leadership principles developed. I highly recommend this book to anyone looking to advance to a higher level of influence through leadership.

—**Zeke Turner**, CEO, Mainstreet

In an age of flawed leadership, where the attitude is often, "Do as I say, not as I do," Dr. Harker challenges leaders (managers, coaches, fathers, mothers, and everyone who has someone who looks up to them) to model the qualities that both exemplify and produce great leaders. Some leadership manuals tend to be gimmicky and/or filled with anecdotes. These may yield immediate results, but unfortunately the effects are frequently transient. In contrast, Dr. Harker's study of leadership is well researched, comprehensive in scope, practical in application, and presented in an impressively succinct fashion. As a result, he offers a prescription that should provide lasting and self-perpetuating effects.

—**Douglas Klendworth, Ph.D.**, Research Chemist, Catalyst Consultant

Dr. Harker's *Leadership Intelligence* is an excellent resource for any leader inside or outside the work environment. He breaks down what goes into building strong leadership qualities by improving "grit." Each section is a great balance of insight, personal experience, and application. I have known Gene for many years and have seen him model leadership. He has taken his experience and research and created a resource to help improve leadership, both professionally and personally.

—**Chas Bowman**, Technical Sales Consultant, Interactive Intelligence

Using his COME UP acrostic, Harker has done a fantastic job of summarizing key characteristics of well-rounded leaders and the psychology behind these characteristics. My personal favorites are "Meaning and Passion," "Do What Matters Most," and "Help others understand the importance of their contribution and find meaning in what they do." Using One Leader's Experience, An Experiment, and Key Concepts summaries at the end of each chapter, the book is geared to any leader wanting to be challenged to take his or her game to the next level.

—**Chris D. Arnold**, Leadership and Life Coach, and Chapter President of Truth@Work

Dr. Gene Harker provides a challenging balance between pragmatism and scholarly thought supported by dependable research. Herein you find fresh thought on the never-ending need for better leaders.

—**Gary York**, Principal, Logicboard, Inc.

There are a lot of books on leadership that discuss the ways we might be more effective with the overwhelming tasks in front of us. These books certainly have their value. What I love and appreciate about Dr. Harker's work on leadership is that he examines the scope of our motivations, passions, and regular routines, suggesting the various ways we might harness those to enhance what he calls our leadership intelligence. Well-researched, thought-provoking, and intensely practical, this important work should be helpful to anyone who desires to make a difference in the lives of others by way of refining their greatest strengths.

—**Aaron Brockett**, Lead Pastor, Traders Point Christian Church

Dr. Gene Harker's *Leadership Intelligence* brings together keen insights and pragmatic exercises in reviewing and expanding contemporary positive psychology. Coming from one who has achieved the highest of success in his profession, been a primary leader in several successful ventures, and consistently developed those whom he leads to high levels of achievement, his is a voice to be heard, understood, and implemented.

—**Tom Foust**, President, SDG International, LLC

In *Leadership Intelligence*, Dr. Harker correlates a variety of facts, rooted in years of research, into a recipe for helping leaders grow in their capacity for influencing others. Serving under his leadership for the past couple of years, I have learned this positive approach by experiencing it in action. In our team, I have watched it help instill a deep sense of resolve in the midst of challenging circumstances.

—**Jennifer Armstrong**, Compliance and Ethics Director for a Fortune 50 insurance and financial services company

Leadership Intelligence has made its way to my bookshelf of great leadership books, wedged between Stephen Covey and Jim Collins. Rooted in the science of positive psychology and lived out in the experiences and stories of real-life leaders, Gene's book fills in the gap between what makes for highly effective individuals and then how those individuals can create teams that are not just good, but great. *Leadership Intelligence* provides an integrated framework for understanding how leaders can model and cultivate excellence in others through positivity, optimism, engagement, and competence. I highly recommend it to anyone looking to bear fruit in the lives of others.

—**Michael L. Tooley**, Partner and Chair, Labor and Employment Group, Ice Miller LLP

Grit has always been here, but Gene Harker pulls it out of obscurity into prominence as the key to leadership intelligence. *Leadership Intelligence* relies on scientific research to reveal a roadmap for leaders to achieve success in any endeavor with a quietly confident sense of well-being. If you are a leader with a bold mission, *Leadership Intelligence* is *your* roadmap.

—**Eric Parmenter, MBA**, Vice President of Employer Solutions, Evolent Health

Reading Dr. Harker's book has provided clarity about the characteristics of the influential people in my life. The people who influence me create a strong desire to achieve my goals, regardless of the constraints and roadblocks I face. As Dr. Harker points out, "A leader's highest priority is helping others thrive by creating a climate that inspires all-out effort in the pursuit of valued goals." *Leadership Intelligence*: *The New Psychology of Grit, Success, and Well-Being* is such a valuable book because it trains one to intentionally and proactively invest in people to bring out their God-given talent.

—**Dwayne Cooper**, Senior Director, GT NEXUS

Having been involved in various leadership arenas over the past 38 years and having read many books on leadership and leaders, I can tell you Gene Harker's *Leadership Intelligence* is not just another book on the topic. As I pored through the pages, thought through the questions, and participated in the surveys, the crystallizing thought in my mind was, "This is becoming *the* leadership book in my library." I eagerly await its publication, for I intend to buy the first 40 copies and hand one to every single person in my workplace. *Leadership Intelligence* will be the wellspring of "grit" for us for years to come.

—**Bill Hoshauer**, Director of Training and Customer Success, Micro Gaming Technologies, Inc.

Dr. Harker explains in (gritty) detail why grit is the key to leadership intelligence and how to live it. He leads you through significant, yet achievable, steps that can positively impact your life and your influence on others. There is much you can ponder and many places you can begin.

—**Dave Tinkey**, Financial Analysis Manager for a large U.S. bank

Every leader asks: "How do I summon the best from my team/employees?" *Leadership Intelligence* offers a positive paradigm that invites the reader to dabble in the provided leadership experiments, thus integrating credible scholarship and practical application. This approach generates a fresh view of the leader, those who are led, and the task at hand. After successful "dabbling," one is motivated to further engage the paradigm. This is a proactive and encouraging piece.

—**Dr. Sherry L. Miller**, General Education Chair and Social Science/Humanities Faculty, Fox College

Dr. Harker's *Leadership Intelligence* is one of the best books on leadership I've read. He doesn't just write about it, he himself demonstrates the qualities he describes in the book. The tools in this book are extremely helpful in quickly assessing one's own leadership intelligence and building a plan for leadership growth.

—**Doug Felton**, Vice President of Corporate Services, The Heritage Group

I have owned and operated three businesses over the last 10 years. The leadership principles discussed in *Leadership Intelligence* by Gene Harker can be applied not only in the workplace but also at home and in our communities. I wish I could have read this book 10 years ago.

—**Ken Julian**, President, Julian Coffee Roasters

Leaders in the emerging digital revolution are seeking a life worth living. Harker's work builds on a few hundred years of research and arrives at a new revelation: leadership intelligence. Peppered with anecdotes and practical application, Harker's book cuts through the noise in the leadership-development space and focuses this powerful, motivational book into a concise, pragmatic field guide for the modern leader. As a builder of teams and companies, I'm looking forward to sharing this work with colleagues and those I mentor. Finally, someone has properly articulated a concept that resonates both with the academic and the leadership practitioner. If you lead or desire to lead, this book should be your next read.

—**Chris Nelson**, CTO, FNEX

In his newest book, *Leadership Intelligence*, Gene Harker presents enduring truths about what it means to lead, and reminds executives, managers, and parents of the tremendous positive influence they have in the lives of others. If you want to be a more effective leader—at work, at home, or in the boardroom—this book will show you how to discover and apply your potential.

—**Kevin Hazelwood**, Vice President and Chief of Staff, Cactus Feeders, Inc.

As a business owner, I was challenged and inspired by this book. Dr. Harker helps us look beyond our reliance on the traditional factors for leadership success and focus on the six characteristics that are precursors to relentless determination and, ultimately, high-level achievement. If you've ever wondered about the secret to getting the most out of yourself and your employees, this is the book for you.

—**Jason Ross**, Managing Partner, Axia Technology Partners

LEADERSHIP
Intelligence

THE NEW PSYCHOLOGY OF GRIT, SUCCESS & WELL-BEING

LEADERSHIP
Intelligence

GENE HARKER

MD PhD

Leadership Intelligence

Copyright © Gene Harker, 2014

All rights reserved. No part of this book may be reproduced, scanned, or distributed in any printed or electronic form without permission. Please do not participate in or encourage piracy of copyrighted materials in violation of this author's rights. Purchase only authorized editions.

ISBN: 978-1-4997-3097-5

Cover design and illustration on pp. 18–19 by Jeff Miller
Typesetting by *www.wordzworth.com*

In memory of my mom, Sharon Harker
Her quiet and compassionate spirit
inspired the very best in everyone she met.

Contents

Preface	i
Grit	**1**
Introduction: Grit	3
A Positive Climate	**21**
1 Competence	25
2 Optimism & Confidence	43
3 Meaning & Passion	67
4 Energy	93
5 Undivided Attention	115
6 Positivity	137
Habit	**155**
Conclusion: Habit	157
Appendices	**163**
Acknowledgements	177
Notes & References	179
About the Author	201

Preface

Born in Scotland to a family of humble means, Andrew Carnegie became one of the wealthiest and most influential leaders of the late 19th and early 20th centuries. In 1848, at age 12, he and his family emigrated to America, initially settling in Allegheny City, Pennsylvania. His first job was as a bobbin boy at a local cotton mill, laboring 12-hour days for about $1 per week. After trying a number of different jobs in the cotton and telegraph industries, at age 17, he began working for the Pennsylvania Railroad as a telegraph operator. From this rather inauspicious beginning, Carnegie rapidly progressed from an employee to an investor, entrepreneur, and business owner. In March 1901, he sold his most successful venture, Carnegie Steel, to United States Steel for $226 million (nearly $169 billion in 2014 dollars) making him the richest man in the world.

One might wonder what contributed to Carnegie's extraordinary success. Could it have been his raw talent? Maybe he was the brightest person in the room. Or perhaps he worked harder than everyone else. While all of these reasons are plausible and likely had something to do with his many achievements, Carnegie himself proposed a different explanation. When queried about the key to his success, he offered a rather humble response, deferring credit to others:

... I will answer your question by saying that we have a Master Mind here in our business, and that mind is made up of more than a score of men who constitute my personal staff of superintendents and managers and accountants and chemists and other necessary types. No one person in this group is the Master Mind of which I speak, but the sum total of the minds in the group, coordinated, organized and directed to a definite end in a spirit of harmonious cooperation, is the power that got my money for me. No two minds in the group are exactly alike, but each man in the group does the thing that he is supposed to do and he does it better than any other person in the world could do it.

Carnegie was keenly aware his success was fundamentally dependent upon others. He realized he was not the hero of even his own success story. His experience taught him that high-level achievement was inextricably linked to his ability to help others identify their strengths and reach their potential. Leadership, for Carnegie, was ultimately about developing human resources, bringing out the best in others.

Despite the American attachment to the romantic ideal of the self-made man or woman, Carnegie's story suggests rugged individualism is not the most common path to meaningful accomplishment. High-level achievement rarely, if ever, results from the effort, even heroic effort, of a single individual. As a general rule, successes, large and small, are ultimately based on the contributions of everyone involved—each person doing what he or she does best.

To thrive in any endeavor, we need one another. Interdependence is part and parcel of the human condition. Many individuals whom we have never met contribute to our lives every day. It's difficult to imagine a world without the creative geniuses who produced the Mona Lisa, light bulb, and iPhone. More directly, we benefit from the support and encouragement offered by teachers, friends, family members, and co-workers. Like Carnegie, we are not the heroes of our own stories. The real hero is the mutually beneficial synergy created when each of us makes our own unique contribution. As Sir Isaac Newton observed, "If I have seen a little further, it is by standing on the shoulders of giants."

When people reach their potential, a positive ripple effect is set in motion. The high school science teacher who just can't wait to get to school in the morning inspires a young scholar who, as an adult, finds a cure for a deadly disease. The computer whiz makes everyone more productive by sharing his expertise. The passion and creativity of a marketing executive changes the whole climate of her department, raising the bar and improving her company's bottom line. When one individual performs well, it's contagious, inspiring others to perform well and ultimately driving organization-wide success.

I frequently wonder what the world has lost because a particular individual failed to reach his or her potential. How many Andrew Carnegies have been born but never quite found their stride? What chemist never developed because she took the wrong turn in life? What invention never made it off the drawing board because a war broke out and the inventor's energies, by necessity, became focused on survival? In my view, if more individuals developed their full potential, there would be less illness, strife, and hunger and more art, creativity, and achievement.

Similarly, I also wonder how many organizations have failed because of an inability to create a climate that calls forth the best in their employees. How many potential Googles, Apples, or Southwest Airlines are not listed among the Fortune 500 because they were unable to inspire their employees to reach their potential? How many companies have significantly underperformed because workers were unable to find meaning and satisfaction in their work? What damage has been done to organizations because of toxic relationships? Could it be that a leader's greatest challenge is not market analysis, strategic planning, or cost containment, but rather it is developing human resources?

This book is about bringing out the best in others. In its pages, I describe a process designed to assist leaders in their efforts to help those they lead reach their full capacity. It is for the CEO who is looking for additional ways to help each individual in her organization thrive. It is for the sales manager who wants to see those he leads not only sell more product but also find meaning in their work. This book is also for the parent who desires to release the potential he sees in his child. It's for leaders of every ilk who believe one of their primary roles is to create a climate that helps others flourish, knowing the success of any group is critically dependent upon individual success.

I call this leadership capacity, this ability to bring out the best in others, *leadership intelligence* (LI). High LI leaders know how to interact relationally in such a way that they inspire friends, family, and colleagues to do their best. They lead in a manner that encourages others to invest, leveraging each person's particular constellation of strengths.

During the past decade, there has been a growing interest in what we, as humans, require in order to thrive in all aspects of life. Researchers in this arena are focusing their efforts on identifying what makes life most worth living. They are studying topics like happiness, pleasure, and satisfaction, as well as optimism, meaning, and hope, searching for the foundations of a good life. Based on this growing body of evidence, we now have a better understanding of what we need emotionally, mentally, socially, and spiritually in order to live a rich, full, meaningful life.

Drawing upon this research, I describe in the pages that follow a process leaders can use to develop their LI. It's a process specifically designed to help leaders create a climate that develops each person's unique potential. This leadership-inspired climate is characterized by positivity, optimism, and engagement. It encourages individuals to seek meaning, find energy, and develop high-quality connections. It's a positive climate that naturally empowers people to develop their capacities.

By developing your LI, a positive organic process is set in motion—one in which the final outcome is difficult to accurately predict. You may encourage an individual who one day becomes a CEO, an elite pianist, or perhaps a Senator. It's more likely, though, that those whose capacities you build won't make headlines. Yet because of our fundamental interdependence, when one individual experiences success, regardless of how success might be defined, others benefit as well. Your efforts to encourage a computer technician, a cellist, or an administrative assistant will have a positive impact on each of them—and all with whom they interact.

Who knows what positivity will ensue when a leader creates a climate in which others find their potential? Those who live a rich, full meaningful life benefit not only themselves, but ultimately their communities. And no one can predict the benefits that may occur one, two, or even three generations from now. When one person wins, everyone wins; individual success is the key to corporate success.

GRIT

Introduction: Grit

Leadership's Highest Priority

Everyone knows on any given day that there are energies slumbering in him which the incitements of that day do not call forth. Compared with what we ought to be, we are only half awake. Our fires are damped, our drafts are checked. We are making use of only a small part of our possible mental and physical resources.

—WILLIAM JAMES

Since 1802, West Point Military Academy has attracted and trained some of the finest young leaders from America and around the world. The admission process to this elite leadership academy is rigorous, with demanding academic and physical standards. Its graduates include a pantheon of great military, government, and business leaders, including U.S. presidents, decorated generals, and successful CEOs.

Each summer, the entering class of cadets at West Point begins its military experience with six weeks of Cadet Basic Training—an experience colloquially known as Beast Barracks. Beast Barracks is physically, emotionally, and mentally challenging. It's likely the most demanding and stressful experience any of these young men and women has faced. Each day begins at 4:45 a.m., and then every minute until 10:00 p.m. is packed with intense training. Cadets do pushups and sit-ups, rappel, navigate obstacle courses, and learn military drills, pushing themselves to the very edge of their mental and physical limits.

As you might expect, not everyone completes the six weeks. On average, about one cadet out of every 20 drops out. In July 2004, 1,218 freshman cadets began Beast Barracks. After six weeks, 71 of these carefully vetted high achievers were no longer a part of the Class of 2008. A study of this class asked the intriguing question: "What was it that differentiated those who persevered from those who did not?" Surprisingly, the answer was not a physical trait like strength or endurance, nor was it a mental trait like intelligence; rather, the answer offered was the character trait *grit*. The cadets highest in grit were 60 percent more likely to complete basic training than their less gritty peers.

Not only is grit essential at West Point, it's essential for almost any endeavor. A number of investigators have observed that it takes, at minimum, 10 years of focused daily practice to become an expert. This 10-year time frame for success is observed so frequently, in so many different settings, it has come to be viewed as a rule—the *10-Year Rule*. For example, there is not a single documented case of a chess player reaching the grandmaster level without a decade of intense practice. Scientists and writers often toil for years before they produce their best work. This rule is also observed in music, mathematics, tennis, swimming, and long-distance running.

Grit is the willingness to do whatever it takes, for however long it takes, to reach one's goals. It's the persistent pursuit of what matters most, regardless of the challenges and setbacks one might face along the way. Without it, no one reaches his or her potential and no organization thrives. Grit is the key to success.

Looking for Success

Though grit is clearly linked to success, it's often overlooked. When seeking a competitive advantage, rather than focusing on persistent effort over time, leaders and organizations commonly focus on talent, experience, and incentives. Schools want the brightest students and businesses look for the most experienced and best talent available. These same schools and businesses develop incentive-based reward systems, hoping to leverage the talent and experience they have worked so hard to attract. Yet while talent, experience, and incentives certainly contribute to success, they have significant limitations.

Talent

It is common to be enamored with what is believed to be natural talent or giftedness. The quarterback with the tight spiral and pinpoint accuracy, the graphic designer with off-the-charts creativity, and the student who's on the dean's list grab our attention. Universities use scores on standardized tests, class rank, and grade-point average as admission criteria, trying to identify those with the ability to excel in the classroom. Organizations search for the best young talent, trying to attract graduates from the most prestigious schools. Businesses are willing to invest a significant portion of their resources in an effort to recruit and retain the brightest and the best.

However, if one takes a closer look, talent is often given too much credit. K. Anders Ericsson, an expert in elite performance, believes that talent is significantly overrated. From his perspective, deliberate practice, not giftedness, is the best predictor of high-level achievement. In his study of world-class violinists, he found that by age 20, top-level violinists had practiced an average of more than 10,000 hours. These top-level violinists practiced approximately 2,500 hours more than the next-most accomplished group of violinists, and 5,000 hours more than the group that performed at the lowest expert level. Similarly, grandmaster chess players spend between 10,000 and 50,000 hours "staring at chess positions," compared to 1,000 to 5,000 hours by less-accomplished players.

While talent is important, it takes a backseat to grit. Success is more a function of persistent effort than innate ability.

Experience

If, as noted above, grit is a better predictor of success than talent, then it would seem all one needs to do is work hard and put in enough time.

However, it's not quite that simple. The person with the most experience is not always the most successful.

Each summer for more than three decades, I have dusted off my golf clubs and headed to the nearest golf course. One would think with all the rounds of golf I've played, I would be an accomplished golfer. Yet, if you have ever seen me hit a golf ball, you know nothing could be further from the truth. At best, my game is consistently mediocre. I have a good bit of experience as a golfer, but that isn't reflected in how well I play.

More on this in Chapter One (*Competence*), but for now, suffice it to say the *type* of experience is as important as the *length* of experience. Experience that consists of doing the same thing over and over again does not improve performance. It's simply more of the same. In contrast, to make progress, one must focus on deficits. Success is found by those who use their time learning new ways to get better at what they do.

Incentives

Along with talent and experience, leaders and organizations rely on rewards as a means for improving performance. Businesses, schools, and groups of all kinds use incentive-based approaches to influence behavior and motivate achievement, believing if one gets the reward system right, one will get the desired results.

At school, performance is rewarded with good grades. At work, if individuals show up and do their job, they receive a paycheck. Performance-based incentives are built on the axiom: Activities that are rewarded increase in frequency, while the frequency of activities that are punished decreases. James Watson, one of the founders of Behaviorism (a rewards-based view of human behavior), once quipped: "Give me a dozen healthy infants, well-formed, and my own specified world to bring them up in and I'll guarantee to take any one at random and train him to become any type of specialist I might select—doctor, lawyer, artist, merchant-chief and, yes, even beggar-man and thief, regardless of his talents, penchants, tendencies, abilities, vocations, and race of his ancestors."

While it's certainly true that work for pay is important and rewards are helpful, they do have limitations. Of particular note, incentives have been shown to decrease motivation and grit. They dampen one's desire to learn, explore, and achieve. This negative impact of rewards on motivation is significant because motivation is one of the best, if not *the* best, predictors of success. People achieve the most when they freely choose activities they find inherently engaging and meaningful. In contrast, those who are motivated to perform based on anticipated rewards feel controlled and tend to do the minimum necessary to receive the promised reward. Individuals engaged because they genuinely enjoy what they are doing receive better grades, are more creative, are more productive in their jobs, and have healthier lifestyles.

A healthcare consultant I know recently told me about an individual she works with who is extraordinarily self-motivated. This employee loves her job. While grateful for her paycheck, it isn't her primary reason for showing up each day. She is compelled by a clear sense of calling. At work, she is known for her can-do attitude—always willing to help out even when it's not her job. Customers seek her out because they know she is willing to listen compassionately and work hard to address concerns. She goes the extra mile, often working past quitting time to make sure everything is done well. Motivated by her passion to make a difference in the lives of those she cares for, she does far more than she is paid to do.

Anyone who is a parent has observed, firsthand, the difference between external rewards and internal motivation. If your child's allowance is based on taking out the trash, cleaning his room, and doing the dishes, he will, if you are lucky, do these assigned chores just often enough and well enough to get his allowance. Not surprisingly, however, when it comes to texting, playing video games, or practicing for a sport he loves, you are required to set limits—because otherwise he would spend all his time doing these activities and nothing else would get done. What's the difference? Chores are forced upon him; he does them to get the desired reward and, of course, get you off his back. Texting, playing, and practicing are activities he loves; he does them because he finds them enjoyable.

When it comes to high-level achievement, choice trumps rewards every time. Success is reserved for those who are fully committed to activities they have freely chosen.

Leaders and organizations that fail to inspire grit, relying instead on talent, experience, and incentives, miss a key element in the success of any individual or team. Individuals achieve at the highest level if, and only if, they are determined to succeed regardless of the effort or cost.

Leadership Intelligence

This book describes how leaders can bring out the best in others by encouraging them to develop a tenacious determination that leads to high-level achievement. Going beyond reliance on talent, experience, and incentives, the pages that follow delineate the activities, conditions, and processes necessary to create a *positive climate* that inspires grit. I call this ability to help others invest and, as a result, reach their potential, *leadership intelligence* (LI).

LI is based on more than a decade of research launched by a keynote address given at an annual meeting of the American Psychological Association. This address, delivered by Martin Seligman, the Zellerbach Family Professor of Psychology at the University of Pennsylvania, called for the development of an expanded focus in the field of psychology—a focus emphasizing our most positive qualities. He challenged psychologists to concentrate their efforts on understanding the things that make our lives fulfilling and productive. Stimulated by Seligman's address, a new field of study has developed under the rubric, positive psychology. Scholars in this field center their efforts on understanding what we, as humans, need to thrive in all aspects of life. Christopher Peterson, a colleague of Seligman, observes: "Positive psychology is the scientific study of what goes right in life, from birth to death and at all steps in between."

As part of my research for this book, I reviewed this growing body of research in order to identify the antecedents of grit and success. My specific objective was to learn about the activities and processes necessary to create a climate that would inspire others to invest, reach their capacity, and perform at the highest level. It was my desire to learn what would motivate a West Point cadet to endure the strenuous challenges of Beast Barracks. I was curious about how to initiate and maintain the effort necessary to put in the thousands of hours required to become a chess master, a violin virtuoso, or an elite athlete.

In addition to reviewing the positive psychology literature, I also enlisted the help of a number of highly respected leaders. I talked with senior management from large, multinational organizations. I met with consultants and professionals who are directing growing enterprises. I spent time with individuals who guide small work teams. I also listened to moms and dads who desire to lead their families well. I selected these individuals because they have one thing in common—all are high LI leaders who are effective in creating a positive climate that inspires engagement and effort.

Based on my conversations with these leaders and my perusal of the positive psychology research, I identified six antecedents of grit and success. These antecedents are qualities or characteristics that, when present, create a climate that inspires and motivates others to fully invest in the pursuit of meaningful endpoints. The first letter of each of these characteristics form the acrostic, *COME UP*:

Competence
Optimism & Confidence
Meaning & Passion
Energy

Undivided Attention
Positivity

These characteristics of a positive climate, when found in groups and organizations, reliably inspire a culture of wholesale buy-in. At the end of this introduction, you will find an illustration summarizing how these characteristics are related to grit and success. This illustration depicts my model of LI and LI's role in helping individuals and organizations flourish.

A Positive Climate: COME UP

In the pages that follow, I dedicate a chapter to each characteristic. A preview is provided below.

Competence

One of the most reliable ways to foster grit is by creating a climate in which individuals are encouraged and empowered to do what they do best. Tasks and projects that utilize a person's strengths naturally engender persistent engagement.

Chapter One, *Competence*, focuses on the identification and development of skills, knowledge, and character strengths. In this chapter, I set individual competencies in the broader context of human development, motivation, and need. I also describe a process for building both team and individual strengths.

Optimism & Confidence

Thoughts influence our actions and feelings. When we approach tasks expecting a positive outcome and believing that we have the requisite skills and resources necessary to succeed, we are more determined and achieve more.

For example, in a fascinating study of the role that confidence plays in persistence, 96 undergraduate students were first exposed to a very difficult task—one at which they were destined to fail. After they had experienced this experimentally induced failure, they were informed that they had done very poorly and that their peers had performed much better. These same participants were then asked to solve another set of problems that they were told were easy to solve. But, in actuality, these problems had no solutions. (How would you like to have been a subject in this experiment? How frustrating!) The investigators then measured how long students persisted at working on this new set of unsolvable problems. What they discovered was that students who had failed on prior problems were less persistent on new ones. In short, they gave up easily because they had lost confidence in their ability to succeed.

Chapter Two, *Optimism & Confidence*, examines the impact of positive thinking on persistence and performance. In this chapter, you will find a process designed to help leaders and the teams they lead develop a can-do mindset.

Meaning & Passion

I spend a significant amount of my time teaching medical students and resident physicians. As their formal education draws to a close, these students and residents enter a stage of life in which they are making important decisions regarding what specialty to pursue and how to shape their professional careers. Appropriately, many of them feel angst regarding their future and the future of their chosen profession. Like most professional school graduates, they will face significant challenges as they leave their training and enter the world of work.

Along with career concerns, many of these young adults are establishing long-term relationships and starting families. As a result, their responsibilities are growing exponentially, and they are beginning to wonder whether it's possible to balance the professional demands and long hours of a medical career with the personal demands of nurturing significant relationships and raising children.

When talking with students or residents who are processing these important matters, I encourage them to think about what they value (meaning) and what they love (passion). Rather than solely fixating on stresses and challenges, I suggest they reflect on why they chose medicine in the first place. I encourage this particular focus because students and residents who view their career as a means for expressing important values achieve more, find greater satisfaction in what they do, and ultimately experience a greater sense of well-being in all aspects of life.

In Chapter Three, *Meaning & Passion*, you will be introduced to a world-renowned psychiatrist who found meaning in the midst of great suffering. You will also meet a software project manager and a department chief. I chose these leaders because all of them, in their own way, are pursuing what they value and what they love. Based on these examples and related research, I propose that meaning and passion produce grit, success, and, ultimately, well-being.

Energy

Energy is a renewable human resource vital to the success of any endeavor. Individuals invigorated by what they do perform better and experience less burnout. They are also more committed to their organizations and are more satisfied. These same employees miss less work and report fewer doctor visits.

This important resource is influenced by a wide variety of personal and environmental factors:

- Self-determination: When we freely choose how to use our time, we accomplish more than when our day is managed by others.
- Connections: Interactions characterized by trust and respect add to the vitality that is experienced; whereas negative exchanges are a drain on morale.
- Breaks: Engagement punctuated by periods of rest and recovery is associated with increased energy and better performance.
- Exercise: Physical activity revitalizes us and contributes to our confidence.
- Nutrition: By eating well, we not only contribute to our health, but fuel our success.
- Sleep: Seven to nine hours of sleep is associated with less fatigue and increased productivity.

In Chapter Four, *Energy*, I describe how you can maximize your own enthusiasm and the enthusiasm of others. Beginning with an energy audit, I delineate a process for building highly focused and engaged teams. By paying attention to factors like job design, positive relatedness, and institutional support you can add to the vitality experienced by the individuals and organizations you lead. The result is an actively engaged team that leverages the talent of each individual and fully utilizes the available resources.

Undivided Attention

A piece of advice frequently offered to children by their parents is "choose your friends wisely." At some point in their young lives, most children hear this parental admonition. (Certainly, I've said it more times than I care to count—just ask my kids.) As it turns out, this advice is important regardless of one's age. The road to success is rarely travelled alone. High-quality connections are potent predictors of personal growth, individual success, and overall well-being.

Leaders who build high-quality connections are in the best position to help others succeed. In fact, without strong relational bonds, one's capacity to lead is severely hampered. Consider your own experience. Perhaps you have observed firsthand the negative impact of incivility. Angry, cutting, and vindictive interactions create instant negativity. All goal-directed, future-oriented activity ceases, and attention is fixated on what just occurred. In contrast, perhaps you have experienced, or are currently experiencing, harmony in your significant relationships. If so, what is the impact on your personal productivity and happiness?

In Chapter Five, *Undivided Attention*, I propose that our ability to influence others is fundamentally determined by our capacity to build high-quality connections. I further suggest that positive interactions are characterized by caring, understanding, appreciating, sharing, and trusting. In addition, we will explore a number of pathways designed to strengthen our relational bonds.

Positivity

Positive emotions prompt action and facilitate engagement. The grandmother who finds joy in interacting with her grandchild will travel across the country just to be near this newfound source of positivity. The satisfaction associated with completing a challenging project compels the research and development team to press on despite significant obstacles. The climber inspired by his sense of wonder can't wait to ascend the next peak.

Investigators, in a study of 229 entrepreneurs and small businesses, found a connection between emotional climate and success. Over an 18-month period, companies with positive leaders experienced greater increases in gross revenue, services offered, customers served, and sales volume than companies whose leaders had a negative bent.

In fact, the companies with a positive emotional climate excelled in all areas of performance that were measured. Similarly, a study of 60 business teams demonstrated that positive teams performed significantly better than negative teams. Teams made up of members who were supportive and encouraging did better on measures of profitability and customer satisfaction. In addition, members of the more upbeat teams were evaluated more favorably by superiors, peers, and subordinates.

Chapter Six, *Positivity*, focuses on our emotions. In this chapter, I propose that we can add positivity to our day by seeking, savoring, and sharing uplifting experiences. I also describe a process for developing a positive emotional climate within the teams that we lead.

The concepts, activities, and processes described in these six chapters are designed to establish a culture of commitment. Leaders who inspire competence, optimism & confidence, meaning & passion, energy, undivided attention, and positivity create a positive climate that brings out the very best in others.

An Added Benefit

While writing this book, I discovered an unexpected, added benefit associated with grit and success. I observed, both in the studies I read and in the lives of the leaders I met, a link between grit, success, and, surprisingly, *well-being*. In short, individuals who work hard at what matters most to them find meaning in what they do and experience a profound sense of personal satisfaction.

In a study of 169 college students, Kennon Sheldon, a widely cited social psychologist and professor of psychology at the University of Missouri, examined the connection between goals, effort, success, and well-being. The students in this study listed 10 personal goals they planned to pursue over the course of a semester. Sheldon also had each participant identify the reason he or she was pursuing each goal. Then, three times during the semester, the students estimated the effort they expended in pursuit of their goals and the progress they were making. In addition, Sheldon measured each student's well-being at the beginning and the end of the semester. Based on what he learned from these students, Sheldon proposed that well-being is an added benefit experienced by those who exert sustained effort in the pursuit of valued goals. The students who set goals they valued exerted more effort, achieved more, and experienced a greater sense of well-being than the students whose goals were less personally meaningful.

Has this been your experience? When you set goals that match your core values, are you more invested and do you achieve more? And does meaningful work add to your positivity and satisfaction?

Leaders who create a climate that inspires effort and high-level achievement are contributing to the well-being of the individuals and teams they lead. Happiness and fulfillment are often found in the determined pursuit of what one cares about most.

The Person in the Mirror

LI begins with you.

At its core, leadership is a personal journey. Those who excel at leading others excel at self-leadership, journeying first where they desire others to follow. If a leader wants followers who listen well, she needs to model undivided attention. The positive emotions of a leader are contagious, spreading to all those he influences. A leader who is all in inspires others to do the same. The person in the mirror is a leader's greatest asset.

In order to develop the characteristics of a positive climate described in this book, you will first need to nurture them in your own life. Once they are internalized, you will be better equipped to cultivate them in others. A significant portion of each chapter is spent on helping you build these characteristics in yourself so you can model them for those who are following your lead.

As you read on, I encourage you to do a series of personal experiments in which you apply the ideas and concepts described in this book. Don't assume or pre-judge. Rather, as you cultivate your LI, simply observe the impact. As you create a positive climate characterized by competence, optimism & confidence, meaning & passion, energy, undivided attention, and positivity, pause to reflect on the impact this climate exerts on the individuals you lead. Are they more engaged? Do they achieve at a higher level? Do they experience a greater sense of personal well-being? And, of equal importance, what is the impact on you?

KEY CONCEPTS

Grit is the key to success

There are no secrets, shortcuts, or three easy steps. Broadly speaking, individuals become what they pursue with passion. While there are physical limits and external realities that place a ceiling on what is possible, the person who persists in the face of obstacles and setbacks has the highest probability of success.

Job one of leadership is bringing out the best in others

A leader's highest priority is helping others thrive by creating a climate that inspires all-out effort in the pursuit of valued goals.

A leader's most important asset is the person in the mirror

LI begins with self-leadership. When it comes to helping others thrive, the primary delivery system is a leader who is thriving.

Everyone is a leader

While this book is primarily focused on leadership in the workplace, it is equally applicable to leadership in other contexts. The father who tutors his child is a leader. The employee encouraging her peers is a leader, helping the whole team and organization succeed. Leadership is not a position or job description; rather it's a way of interacting that brings out the best in others.

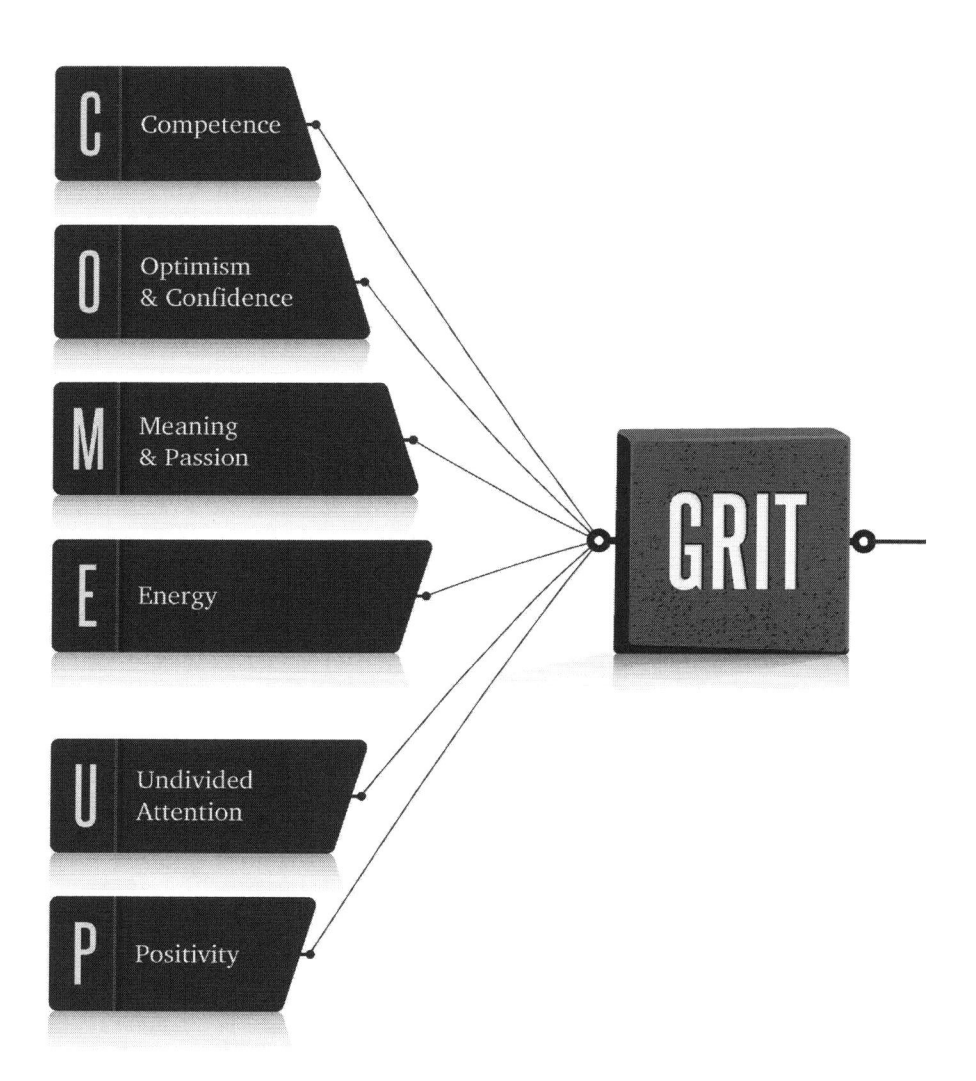

- **C** — Competence
- **O** — Optimism & Confidence
- **M** — Meaning & Passion
- **E** — Energy
- **U** — Undivided Attention
- **P** — Positivity

GRIT

LEADERSHIP Intelligence

A POSITIVE CLIMATE

C
O
M
E

U
P

Competence
C O M E U P

ONE

Competence

Do What You Do Best

> *... the master lever is getting each person to play to his strengths. Pull his lever, and an engaged and productive team will be the result. Fail to pull it, and no matter what else is done to motivate the team, it'll never fully engage. It will never become a high-performance team.*
>
> —Marcus Buckingham

I just want to get better!

Debbi, a mom with two grown children, was in severe pain—a demotivating pain that for most would be all consuming. Despite multiple trips to the doctor, her pain continued to escalate. Yet on this particular day, she insisted on attending her art class at a local university. She wouldn't miss it. Regardless of the intensity of her discomfort, her desire to grow as an artist compelled her to go.

Debbi has remarkable grit. When it comes to developing her artistic abilities, she is all in—nothing dissuades her. I asked Debbi to describe the source of her motivation and the factors that have helped her improve:

I have always loved art—especially drawing and painting. For as long as I can remember, art has brought me nothing but joy. Early in life, I began to appreciate color, textures, and images. I saw beauty everywhere I looked.

I have a deep, inexplicable drive to improve as an artist. From somewhere within, I have an irresistible desire to realize the artistic capacity God has placed in my heart and mind. Seeing myself improve really gets me going. When I complete a project, I experience a profound sense of fulfillment and satisfaction. And, certainly, the drive I feel to hone my artistic skills comes from the encouragement I receive from others. I am grateful for friends, family, and even folks I don't know who look at my work and offer their kind words of support. The fact that others take an interest in what I do is profoundly meaningful and motivating.

I am most grateful for the many opportunities I have had to work on my skills as an artist. The most helpful of these opportunities began several months ago when I started taking an oil painting course at a nearby university. It had been 35 years since I had any formal instruction—raising a family has a way of forcing one to put things on hold. In this class, I am getting great instruction and useful feedback.

I demand a lot of myself. I set the bar high and love the challenge of creating ever-improving works of art. I'm always creating. Regardless of where I am, whether I'm in the car (not while driving, of course), at our children's homes, in restaurants, or on vacation, I'm constantly practicing.

Debbi's quest for competence is quite remarkable. She spends the majority of her free time learning about art, seeking expert instruction, practicing, practicing, and then practicing some more. The result is beautiful art, a realized potential, and a profound sense of personal satisfaction.

Competence, the pursuit of excellence, is an innate human motivation. From birth, children are natural explorers. They exhibit a clear predilection to learn about the world in which they live and to develop more and more complex competencies. The American philosopher John Rawls calls this fundamental motivation *The Aristotelian Principle*. He writes: "The Aristotelian Principle states that, other things equal, human beings enjoy the exercise of their realized capacities (their innate or trained abilities), and that this enjoyment increases the more the capacity is realized, or the greater its complexity." People find great satisfaction in reaching their potential. There is an inner "I just want to get better" that drives human thought and action. Mastery is its own reward.

According to the developmental psychologist Erik Erikson, children from age six to the onset of puberty who develop a sense of competence fare better than those who fail to do so. Children in this age group are presented with a number of social, intellectual, and physical challenges:

Social: As they mature, they are required to become adept at getting along with others, navigating the subtleties and complexities of human social interaction. They learn to relate to an ever-widening circle of adults and peers.

Intellectual: In their classrooms, they are confronted with a variety of academic subjects they must master. Along with the required subjects, many of them become interested in the fine arts and start taking private lessons to foster their nascent artistic talent.

Physical: During this developmental period of life, children are introduced to a wide-range of physical activities like soccer, basketball, and ballet.

Those who successfully meet these challenges become relentless explorers who actively seek opportunities to learn. Unfortunately, those who experience repeated failure are prone to develop a sense of inferiority. And, as a result, they disengage, avoiding further academic, social, and physical opportunities for growth.

Richard Ryan and Edward Deci, architects of Self-Determination Theory (see Chapter 4, *Energy*), consider competence a basic human need. They suggest well-being is a byproduct of putting in the hard work necessary to reach one's potential. Like a plant needs water, sunlight, and nutrients from the soil, competence is required for maximum personal fulfillment.

Rawls' moral philosophy, Erikson's model of development, and Ryan and Deci's Self-Determination Theory all suggest that those of us who exert the effort needed to build competencies are the ones who will thrive. These philosophers and scholars suggest competence is part and parcel of the good life.

This view of the good life contradicts the conventional wisdom that humans are primarily motivated to seek pleasure and avoid pain. Conventional wisdom suggests "take it easy, avoid hard work, indulge your senses, and do what feels good." This wisdom implies that, all things being equal, most would choose the quick fix—the path of least resistance. In contrast, an approach that places competence at the center of motivation, development, and need fulfillment suggests the way to happiness is through grit. Not a masochistic seeking of pain without purpose, but a determined effort focused on getting better.

How does this square with your experience? When you complete a challenging task at work, does it get your juices flowing? When you run your personal best in a 5K, do you experience a sense of accomplishment? Do you receive more lasting pleasure from a week on the beach or completing a difficult task that required months of effort?

Competence

Competence is a key component of the life well lived. It contributes directly to our satisfaction, well-being, and performance:

Satisfaction: Gregory Berns, a researcher at Emory University, has extensively studied the neurobiology of satisfaction. Based on his research, he has localized this positive emotion to a region of the brain called the striatum. He observes: "Deep in your brain is a structure that sits at the crossroad of action and reward. Based on a decade of study, I have found that this region, which may hold the key to satisfaction, thrives on challenge and novelty." Berns suggests that individuals who succeed at meeting difficult challenges experience a profound sense of satisfaction. By putting in the long hours required to build requisite competencies, the marathoner, computer programmer, and dancer all add to their pleasure and long-term fulfillment.

Well-Being: In a study of college students, the investigators observed that daily fluctuations in well-being were closely tied to competence. On each of 14 consecutive days, participants in the study were asked to rate how proficient they felt with respect to the activities they participated in. Students who felt competent were less negative, more energetic, and reported fewer physical complaints.

Performance: Over the past several years, researchers from the Gallup organization have written extensively regarding the role of strengths (competencies) in improving the performance of individuals and organizations. Based on their findings, these researchers have identified a clear link between using one's strengths and success. For example, Gallup researchers studied a timeshare company's sales force. In this group of professionals, those who received feedback on their strengths had an 11 percent increase in sales. Similarly, in a Gallup survey of 7,939 business units in 36 companies, business units in which employees were afforded the opportunity to do what they do best experienced lower turnover, greater productivity, and higher customer satisfaction scores.

In short, individuals who identify and use their competencies get the most out of life. They work hard, find satisfaction, and achieve at a high level.

Deliberate Practice

In the movie *Groundhog Day*, Phil (Bill Murray) is a self-absorbed, cynical weatherman from Pittsburgh assigned, for the fourth year in a row, to cover the Groundhog Day celebration on Feb. 2 in Punxsutawney, Pennsylvania—an assignment he feels is well beneath his sophistication and prodigious talent. He is accompanied on this assignment by a cameraman, Larry (Chris Elliott) and a newly hired producer, Rita (Andie MacDowell). Rita is a young, attractive, and truly genuine person who possesses an unwavering confidence in the goodness of others and a positive outlook on life. Predictably, Phil and Rita clash, with Phil responding to Rita's innocence and optimism with sarcasm and cutting humor.

The story takes an unexpected turn when, inexplicably, Phil begins to relive the same day, Groundhog Day, over and over again. Day after day, he awakens to the same song playing on his clock radio, meets the same people, and has the same conversations. At first, Phil's flaws are accentuated by his fate. He begins to live in excess, eating whatever he wants, stealing, driving recklessly, and seeking a series of one-night-stands. He makes multiple attempts to seduce Rita, but she rebuffs his advances.

Over time, however, there is an evolution in Phil's attitude. He begins to live each day to better himself and better the lives of those around him. He reads classical literature, learns a foreign language, and takes piano lessons. He uses his foreknowledge of events to catch a boy falling from a tree, change a flat tire, and perform the Heimlich maneuver to save a man choking on his dinner. Rather than repeating the same day and the same activities over and over again, he begins to benefit from his experiences, leveraging each day to become a better person. And, as in all good stories, after his change of heart he gets the girl, the time problem resolves, and he wakes up on Feb. 3.

It's often assumed that experience is the best teacher. The manager with 10 years on the job is believed to be more competent than the manager with five years of work experience. Common sense suggests that the seasoned analyst should perform better than the one fresh out of graduate school. Yet, as depicted in the movie *Groundhog Day*, experience alone does not inevitably result in better performance—sometimes experience is nothing more than more of the same.

A number of researchers have noticed a disconnect between experience and performance. For example, the authors of a study published in *Harvard Business Review* observed that senior managers were less able to adapt. These experienced managers stuck with initial time, cost, and production estimates even when they were made aware these initial estimates were unrealistic. The authors concluded that in some situations less-experienced employees perform better.

Similarly, based on their review of 62 published studies, researchers from Harvard Medical School observed that more experienced physicians don't always provide better health care. Specifically, they noted that "... physicians who have been in practice for more years and older physicians possess less factual knowledge, are less likely to adhere to appropriate standards of care, and may have poorer patient outcomes." Yikes!

Likewise, mental health professionals' clinical performance isn't necessarily related to experience. In one study, psychiatrists were asked to make a diagnosis based on initial interviews with patients at the time of their hospital admission. Interestingly, in this group of clinicians, diagnostic accuracy was not related to the number of years in practice—less-experienced psychiatrists did just as well as the more experienced ones. In another study, based on information from a psychological test, individuals with four levels of training were asked to determine whether a child required psychiatric treatment. Surprisingly, in this study, psychiatry interns had the same diagnostic accuracy as ward secretaries. And the individual with the lowest accuracy was a highly trained expert.

Taken alone, these studies suggest a competitive advantage would be gained by firing senior employees, finding a doctor who is fresh out of residency, and giving up on the efficacy of psychiatry. However, this interpretation isn't totally justified, because these studies don't tell the whole story. They only look at the *length* of experience. What is missing is an examination of the *kind* of experience.

Experience that is more of the same is just that—more of the same. It's ineffective at improving performance. In contrast, experience focused on continuous improvement results in better performance. K. Anders Ericsson, who has spent his entire professional career studying experts, suggests experience contributes to competence when individuals are motivated to work hard at getting better, given instruction regarding what needs to improve, open to feedback about performance deficits, and willing to practice skills that need improvement. He calls this approach to continuous improvement, *deliberate practice*.

According to Ericsson, experience leads to competence and success when it's motivated by a desire to improve. Individuals who are determined to get better turn their experiences into opportunities for growth. Driven by a passion to learn, they strive to mitigate weaknesses and build strengths.

Along with a desire to improve, competence requires instruction. Guidance from others is a prerequisite for getting better at most any skill. Sales professionals, software designers, and parents benefit from expert outside input designed to sequence learning and ameliorate deficits. Without this kind of input, performance tends to level off and experience becomes ineffectual—more of the same. The participants in a study of memory were taught a mnemonic device designed to enhance their ability to recall a list of 30 unrelated words. After a period of instruction in which the mnemonic was taught, the performance of these participants increased dramatically. Prior to instruction, the young adults in this study remembered an average of 7.6 words. After instruction, they remembered 28.7 words. Memory, like any skill, is enhanced by proper instruction.

As individuals begin to change what they do as a result of the instruction they receive, feedback is required to further refine performance. Ericsson observed: "In the absence of adequate feedback, efficient learning is impossible and improvement only minimal even for highly motivated individuals." The importance of immediate, personalized, and ongoing feedback has been demonstrated in studies that examine teaching methods. In these studies, tutored students performed better than 98 percent of students taught in traditional classrooms. In addition, tutored students spent about 90 percent of their instruction time working on academic content while students in conventional classrooms spent about 65 percent of their time actively learning. To perform at their best, individuals, regardless of their job or role in life, need focused feedback.

Motivation, instruction, and feedback are only effective when accompanied by an approach to practice that intentionally focuses on continuous improvement. The athlete who wants to improve at his sport works on the weaknesses in his game. In order to hone her skills, the musician practices the difficult sections of her growing repertoire—again and again until it's automatic. By focusing on what mentors, supervisors, or coaches identify as weaknesses in performance, individuals are able to consistently improve performance and add new competencies. In the words of legendary Green Bay Packers' coach Vince Lombardi, "Practice does not make perfect. Only perfect practice makes perfect."

For the past few years, I have maintained a fairly consistent exercise regimen. I do the same workout most mornings. As a result, my routine is automatized; I can do it without thought. While this routine makes a valuable contribution to my health, I don't progress because I do the same exercises every day. Contrast this with my nephew, Isaac, the quarterback for his high school football team. To get better, he receives instruction from leading professionals who teach him what he needs to do to excel. They explain and demonstrate every detail of expert performance, like how to drop back from center, where to fix his gaze, and how to hold the football. They cover every detail. Once he knows precisely what to do, he performs the behavior under the watchful eyes of his instructors. When they identify an error, Isaac is given immediate feedback. He practices proper technique until it becomes automatic. As a result, he is steadily improving.

Without deliberate attention to continuous improvement, individuals stop progressing. I have seen this happen on countless occasions. Individuals in every line of work settle into a routine and, as a result, their performance plateaus or, worse, declines. The development and maintenance of competencies requires motivation, instruction, feedback, and practice—all intentionally focused on learning and achieving at the highest level.

Leader Competencies

As a leader, building your own competencies is the first step in helping others build theirs. Competencies are what you enjoy doing and what you do well. They are your strengths and passions. These are the activities and projects you are naturally drawn to—what you think about when you get up in the morning and what keeps you up at night.

To help develop your competencies, begin by taking a personal inventory. Make a list of the activities you like and are good at. When making this list, focus on skills, knowledge, and characteristics.

What skills have you acquired? Do you have expertise in developing software, greeting customers, or encouraging your children to excel?

Skills are anything you do that sets you apart—the activities others see as your strengths.

Along with skills, add to your list areas in which you are knowledgeable. Have you spent time learning about mathematics, French cuisine, or market trends? Most any area of knowledge can lead to a competency. Don't be too analytical—simply list anything that comes to mind.

Then, in addition to skills and knowledge, add personal characteristics to your list. You have traits that make you who you are. These traits are the competencies that influence how you approach things. Identifying them is difficult because they are abstract, complex, and nuanced.

To help with this, consider a list of 24 character strengths developed by Christopher Peterson from the University of Michigan. His list includes personal attributes like creativity, curiosity, authenticity, bravery, and zest. It's available online at viacharacter.org. You can begin generating your list of character competencies by simply perusing Peterson's list to see if you resonate with any of them. Do any of them describe you? Which ones are most characteristic of the way you interact with others? If you desire to take this a step further, the website identified above also includes a free online survey you can use to identify your top character strengths.

As you add items to your list of competencies, begin paying attention to how each of them is expressed in the course of your day. How do you use your knowledge of international law? When do you apply your communication skills? How does your positivity find expression? For each of the competencies you have listed, identify specific ways you are currently using them. Further, pay attention to how you feel when exercising a particular competency. Does it energize you? When expressing it, do you feel a sense of satisfaction?

To further refine your list, consider sharing it with a few friends, select family members, or colleagues who know you well. See if they agree with the items on your list. Individuals you interact with on a regular basis are in the perfect position to see you at your best. They are able to share anecdotes about instances in which your skills, knowledge, and characteristics were perfectly matched to a particular situation. In addition, they may see strengths in you that you don't see in yourself.

As your list takes shape, start considering how you might use your competencies more regularly. They are like any skill you possess; without deliberate practice your performance plateaus.

To build your competencies focus on …

Motivation: Improvement begins with a felt desire to get better. Start with the skills, knowledge, and characteristics you are most passionate about. What are you drawn to do? What competencies would you like to develop?

Instruction: It's difficult to get better without outside input. If you have a current competency you desire to improve or a new one you would like to develop, enlist the help of others who have the requisite skill and knowledge to offer needed instruction. That instruction can come from a variety of sources—from a teacher in a classroom or workshop, for instance, or from written sources, instructional videos, or individual coaching.

Feedback: The most accurate and useful feedback is based on direct observation. As you develop competencies, when possible, arrange for others to observe what you are doing. If you are a sales professional, from time to time have someone sit in as you work with a customer, in order to offer input on your approach. If you are designing a website, ask an expert for suggestions to make it better. In general, the most beneficial feedback is immediate and provides detailed information regarding what needs to improve.

Practice: There is no substitute for repetition that addresses deficits. Take the information and feedback you receive and use it to improve performance—not more of the same, but practice with the intent of getting better.

Once you have identified your competencies and are working to develop them, look for ways to use them in as many settings as possible. Leverage your strengths. Do what you do well and then observe the impact. Are you more satisfied and energetic? Do you accomplish more in less time?

Team Competencies

Researchers from the Gallup organization have observed that teams are more likely to demonstrate grit when their strengths are being used to the fullest extent possible. In one Gallup study, when leaders ignored their employees, 40 percent of those workers disengaged. When leaders focused on weaknesses, 22 percent disengaged. However, when leaders spent their time focusing on employee strengths, only 1 percent of their employees disengaged.

As a leader, you help team members develop their competencies when you …

Know Individual Competencies: Get to know the strengths of the individuals you lead. Identify the skills, knowledge, and characteristics each person possesses. What is it that sets a particular individual apart? What does each person do well and what is he or she passionate about?

Build Teams Based on Competencies: Use your knowledge of individual competencies to build and task your teams. Place individuals on teams based on a match between the strengths they offer and the requirements of a given project. If you need coordinated effort, add individuals who communicate well and have a history of working well with others. If computer skills are required, find a person who can bring these skills to the table. There is a synergy that occurs when each team member is working in his or her area of competence.

Encourage the Use of Competencies: Challenge each person to leverage his or her strengths, doing what he or she does best as often as possible. Put everyone in a position to succeed. The more individuals are able to use their competencies in a given day, the harder they work and the more they accomplish.

Strengthen Current Competencies: Don't settle for the status quo. Provide the instruction and feedback necessary to help each team member improve. Create an environment rich with learning opportunities.

Develop New Competencies: When individuals focus too much on current strengths, stagnation occurs and opportunities for growth are missed. There is an inherent satisfaction in taking on new challenges. Encourage team members to develop new competencies—ones that will complement their current ones and add to their sense of achievement.

The cultivation of competence is a powerful means for facilitating engagement. Team members who are doing what they love and what they do well are naturally all in. There is no need to micromanage, exhort, or incentivize. It's simply not necessary.

One Leader's Experience

Mike is a successful attorney whose LI is off the charts. He is uniquely able to create a positive climate that inspires grit, success, and well-being. I asked Mike to reflect on his own competencies, as well as how he develops them in others:

Question 1: What are your greatest competencies/strengths? What do you do to improve in your areas of competence? How do you use your competencies at work and/or in your personal life?

I try to take (or re-take) competency tests every few years to gain a better sense for how I'm wired and to see how I'm changing over time. The most recent StrengthsFinder test I took in May of 2010 identified my top five strengths as Relator, Learner, Strategic, Developer, and Individualization, in that order. The StandOut test I took in 2011 ranked me highest in the following two areas: "Creator: You make sense of the world, pulling it apart, seeing a better configuration, and creating it." And "Connector: You are a catalyst. Your power lies in your craving to put two things together to make something bigger than it is now."

A slightly different question would be, "What are the competencies/strengths that distinguish me or give me the greatest competitive advantage?" As a lawyer at a big law firm that attracts lawyers from high-ranking schools, there is a certain amount of natural intelligence and hard work that goes along with being successful (the "price of admission," if you will). What makes me different and gives me a competitive advantage are two things: (1) My greatest strength is an ability to recognize the unique gifts that each person brings to the team/firm/group; and (2) I have a low individual ego but high team ego that allows me to feel the best when I'm promoting others and helping them succeed. These two characteristics cause me to get an unusual amount of satisfaction out of managing and developing others from behind the scenes.

I have not had the benefit of anyone trying to develop or "grow" me for at least the past 15 years; so, I've been forced to become self-taught. I read books about developing myself and others, I look for opportunities to do presentations and write articles about those subjects, and I sprinkle the things I learn into conversations with clients, colleagues, and friends. I treat a new book or a new idea like a fine bottle of wine and tell people whom I value about it so that they can enjoy it as well. At home, I try to use my competencies to become a better husband and father by acknowledging the things that make my wife and children unique and encouraging them to develop their gifts.

Question 2: How do you help the individuals you lead identify, develop, and use their competencies?

I first have to get to know them well in order to make sure I understand their wiring, as opposed to having a superficial understanding of their competencies. At the same time, I try to develop the sort of relationship with them that causes them to believe I'm more interested in helping them than in helping myself at their expense. Once those two things happen, I will (a) articulate the things that I've observed them being particularly good at to see if they're in agreement, (b) express a vision for how I can see them using those competencies, (c) if they're receptive, look for opportunities that match up with their competencies, (d) share the positive results of their competencies with them and the larger team, and (e) periodically identify obstacles I see that are getting in the way of their using their competencies to the fullest.

An Experiment

Below is an exercise designed to help you and the individuals you lead cultivate competencies. Let me suggest you approach this exercise as an experiment. After trying it for a week, determine its impact on you and those you lead. Does cultivating competencies make a difference in your satisfaction, well-being, and performance? Are those you lead more engaged, productive, and happy?

Your Competency

- Choose one of your competencies. Pick the one you are most motivated to work on.
- Find ways to improve your performance. Gather information and solicit feedback that will help you get better.
- Use this competency every day for the next week. Find unique and creative ways to employ it in as many settings as possible.

Team Competency

- Select a team member.
- Identify one of his or her competencies.
- Provide information and feedback to improve his or her performance.
- Ask him or her to use this competency every day for a week.

KEY CONCEPTS

Competence is central to the life well lived

We are born with a desire to grow. When we cultivate this innate desire, we are more engaged, productive, and satisfied.

Deliberate Practice is the key to developing competencies

Unless we consistently work at getting better, plateaus in performance are inevitable. Being our best requires practice that is focused on continuous improvement.

C
Optimism & Confidence
M
E
U
P

TWO

Optimism & Confidence

The Power of Can-do

The mind is its own place, and in itself
Can make a Heaven of Hell, a Hell of Heaven.

—John Milton

Fresh out of graduate school, Alex moved to Washington, D.C. to begin his professional career. After looking for a few weeks, he saw a job opening that interested him, submitted a resume, and secured a phone interview. At the end of the interview, a face-to-face meeting was scheduled for the following day, where, among other things, the potential employer would ask Alex to demonstrate competence using InDesign, a desktop publishing software application. He had his foot in the door and was excited about the opportunity, but there was one challenge: While he had used similar software programs, he had never used this particular one. Undaunted, Alex went to work. He Googled instructional videos and spent the remainder of the day learning InDesign's capabilities. The next day he showcased his newly acquired skill, aced the interview, and secured the job.

Alex approached this employment opportunity like he approaches all of life, with a can-do attitude. He believed he could acquire, in a very short period of time, the knowledge and skill he needed. Without a belief in his ability to succeed, he might have walked away. Instead, buoyed by optimism and confidence, Alex placed himself in a situation where securing a job was not only possible but probable. Positive thinking gave him a clear advantage.

A number of years ago, Martin Seligman and a colleague conducted two studies that highlight the remarkable impact of positive thought patterns like those Alex demonstrated. These investigators examined the connection between optimism, workplace productivity, and employee retention in a group of insurance agents. In the first study, they found that optimistic agents were the most productive, selling 37 percent more than their pessimistic peers. The second study examined 104 recently hired agents. In this group of new hires, optimism predicted which agents were still working at the end of one year as well as which of them were the most productive. Twice as many optimistic agents were still on the job after the first year, and the most optimistic new hires sold 57 percent more than pessimistic ones.

These studies and scores of others provide compelling evidence that the way we think about our situation, our future, and ourselves has a powerful impact. We are not mindless automatons helplessly reacting to stimuli in our environment. In fact, the opposite is true; we are active shapers of our world. Our ability to think gives us the capacity to anticipate the impact of a given course of action. And as a result, we can influence what happens by choosing the course we believe will give us the best chance for success. Because we can mentally process information, we don't have to learn everything by trial and error. By watching what others do, we can model our behavior after theirs; or if we believe their actions are ineffective, we can choose a different path. As thinking beings, we can decide to persist in our efforts to reach goals even in the face of seemingly insurmountable odds. In short, our minds give us the capacity to be active, choosing agents in life; not simple cause-and-effect machines.

In this chapter, I describe a process for developing, in ourselves and in others, a can-do mindset. This mindset is based on *optimism* and *confidence*—two familiar and widely studied patterns of thinking. Research and our own experience tells us that when we believe we can execute a particular course of action (confidence) and when we expect a good result (optimism), we are much more likely to excel in our pursuits. In fact, a can-do attitude is one of the most reliable sources of grit, success, and well-being.

Optimism

Optimism consists of positive mental *expectations* and *explanations*. Optimists expect a good day today and an even better one tomorrow. They anticipate their efforts will be rewarded with achievement and success. When taking a college course, they assume it will go well. When seeking a promotion, they are confident they will get the job. This perspective is a source of motivation for optimists, enabling them to consistently meet the challenges that come their way.

In addition to positive expectations, optimists offer positive explanations for the circumstances they encounter:

- They experience a sense of control over the good in life, assuming a causal connection between their actions and outcomes.
- They trust that good fortune will continue. Positive outcomes are normative—a stable part of their life.
- They believe success in one area of their life will generalize to other areas as well.

When an optimistic executive makes a successful presentation, she attributes her success to ability and hard work. And she trusts she will continue to do well.

Optimists have characteristic ways of explaining setbacks:

- Recognizing many problems are caused by factors beyond their control, they aren't too self-critical. They don't overly personalize negative experiences or internalize an inordinate amount of blame.

- They believe a bad experience is not likely to repeat itself or last forever. Negative events are viewed as short-lived setbacks, not lasting catastrophes.
- Optimists don't overgeneralize. They are able to compartmentalize, believing a bad outcome in one area of their life doesn't mean bad things will happen in other areas.

If an optimistic marketing executive fails to secure an important account, he doesn't become his own worst enemy. He learns from his mistakes and moves on, believing he will do better the next time.

In contrast to their optimistic peers, pessimists offer very different explanations of both positive and negative experiences:

- When pessimists experience a positive event, they attribute it to factors beyond their control—good is the result of random fortuitous events.
- They believe success is a short-lived anomaly, not likely to occur again. Positive outcomes are viewed as transient occurrences unrelated to personal effort or actions.
- A positive event is an isolated incidence that doesn't have a broader impact.

The pessimistic manager views his recent success as a happenstance, being in the right place at the right time. He is simply the benefactor of a lucky turn of events. There wasn't much he could have done to influence the outcome.

When pessimists have negative experiences, they tend to think …

- *It's all my fault*: Pessimists accept too much personal blame. They are merciless self-critics. Negative events are believed to be the direct result of their perceived ineptitude.
- *It's going to last forever*: They believe difficulties persist. When faced with unwanted challenges, they can't see an end to their troubles.
- *It's going to undermine everything*: Individuals with a negative bent overgeneralize failure. If they struggle in one area, they assume they

will struggle in other areas as well. Setbacks are viewed as global indictments of their ability and worth.

As a result of this characteristic way of thinking, pessimists experience a disconnect between effort and reward, assuming no matter what they do or how hard they work they have little control over outcomes. This perceived disconnect predictably leads to a sense of helplessness. The IT director who fails to meet a deadline catastrophizes, thinking the next project won't be any better, his whole career is ruined, and he is entirely to blame. This pessimistic bent erodes his confidence and causes him to disengage from projects at work.

Clearly, when these competing ways of thinking are studied in the workplace, optimism is the winner. Employees who expect the best are more productive, more satisfied with their jobs, and less likely to quit. They are less cynical and exhibit fewer counterproductive behaviors. Optimistic employees are more likely to work well with others and are more committed to the organizations they serve.

The way optimists approach setbacks is one of their greatest assets. They are active problem solvers, perceiving obstacles to success as challenges, consistently asking themselves "Where's the opportunity in this difficulty?" They address problems directly with concrete, action-oriented solutions. These positive thinkers have grit, resisting any barrier that might subvert their efforts to reach desired objectives.

Optimists also make better emotional adjustments to circumstances beyond their control:

- They frame difficulties in the best possible light, looking for the benefit in even the most challenging situation.
- They are adept at using humor to alleviate stress and lighten the moment.
- Optimists view setbacks as learning experiences, which can be leveraged to improve future decision-making.

- In the midst of challenges, they seek support from friends and family, appropriately utilizing resources in their social network.

All of these actions help optimists adjust emotionally to the slings and arrows of outrageous fortune that come their way.

Pessimists, on the other hand, take a very different approach to the challenges they face:

- They tend to deny difficulties, hoping they will go away if they're ignored.
- They disengage from problems and stop investing in solutions.
- When faced with adversity, pessimists withdraw from others, separating themselves from potential support.

Charles Carver and Michael Scheier, widely cited leaders in optimism research, summarize the differences between the problem-solving strategies of optimists and pessimists with these words: "In general, optimists tend to use more problem-focused coping strategies than do pessimists. When problem-focused coping is not a possibility, optimists turn to strategies such as acceptance, use of humor, and positive reframing. Pessimists tend to cope through overt denial and by mentally and behaviorally disengaging from the goals with which the stressor is interfering."

In addition to having a positive impact on productivity, it has long been acknowledged that optimism contributes to health and well-being. In a study of Harvard University graduates (classes of 1942-1944), the investigator observed a link between pessimism and poor health. When the participants in this study were 25 years of age, they were asked a series of questions about difficulties they had experienced while in active military duty during World War II. The graduates who offered pessimistic responses to these questions had the most health problems over the course of their lifetime.

The health benefits of optimism are not limited to Harvard graduates. Optimists do better following surgery, experience less depression, and are less likely to develop heart disease. They are less stressed, less depressed, less lonely, and have more social support.

Optimism has also been linked to longevity. In one study, investigators examined newspaper quotes made by Hall of Fame baseball players during their playing days. Some of these highly successful professional athletes were optimistic, saying things like …

- "… nothing but the breaks beat me in that first game, but I never complain about that for I feel that things square themselves, and I'll get my share the next time."
- "Confident we'll even things tomorrow … we are hitting."

Others were more pessimistic, remarking …

- "… those guys were just too good for us."
- "The most unusual part of this is that this is the first series in which I haven't felt inspired. I just don't seem to give a darn what happens. It's no longer life and death. I saw enough of that in the war."

Amazingly, players with optimistic quotes lived longer than those whose quotes were pessimistic. It's remarkable that a few words spoken to a reporter during one's youth can predict longevity.

The data is clear: regardless of profession or station in life, optimism offers a clear advantage.

Confidence

In the mid-1970s, Albert Bandura proposed a theory to explain why we do what we do (human behavior). One of the key components of this theory is a concept called self-efficacy. At its core, self-efficacy refers to our belief in our ability to perform a particular task. Bandura's theory focuses on beliefs rather than skills, hypothesizing that confidence produces actions that result in desired outcomes. When we trust in our capacity to perform the tasks necessary to reach a goal, we are more likely to succeed.

Self-efficacy (*i.e.* confidence) is a characteristic way of thinking. It's an *a priori* belief that a particular job is doable. It's a programmer's thoughts regarding his capacity to complete the tasks necessary to successfully initiate and finish a new project. It's the young lawyer's positive expectation she has what it takes to pass the bar. Individuals high in self-efficacy are confident, believing they can execute a particular behavior; while individuals low in self-efficacy lack confidence, believing they can't do what they need to do in order to succeed.

It's worth noting that confidence is task specific. We all feel different levels of confidence depending on the particular activity being considered. We might be very sure in our ability to make a sales pitch but doubt our ability to enter data into a spreadsheet. We may believe we are quite capable of writing code for a complex software program but feel very anxious when considering the prospect of presenting our ideas to a supervisor. Each of us has our own constellation of tasks we approach with confidence and ones we approach with trepidation.

Like optimism, confidence contributes to better performance and better health:

Better Performance: In one study, investigators examined how self-assurance affected job performance and job attitudes in a group of telecommunications service technicians. Technicians in this study who believed in their capacity to succeed were more satisfied, more committed to their jobs, and more productive. They missed fewer days of work and were on time more often.

Other studies have shown that confidence contributes to creativity and leadership ability. Individuals who believe in themselves are also more persistent when faced with difficult tasks. In one comprehensive review, the authors suggest that confidence contributes more to work performance than goal setting or job satisfaction.

Better Health: Not only does confidence contribute to performance, it also adds to personal health and well-being. For example, confident individuals adapt better to illness. In a study of patients with rheumatoid arthritis, it was noted that patients who believed they could cope well with their disease reported less pain and fatigue, while experiencing improved general health, better physical functioning, and increased vitality. Further, in patients with heart disease, those who doubted their ability to deal with their illness experienced more problematic symptoms, greater physical limitations, worse quality of life, and an overall decline in health. Confidence has also been shown to benefit individuals suffering with diabetes, cancer, and chronic pain.

In addition, positive beliefs in one's ability are a resource for individuals trying to change their health habits. Confident individuals are more successful when it comes to smoking cessation, weight control, and exercise maintenance. In a study of college students, a link was found between self-assurance and an increased likelihood of engaging in positive health-related activities including spiritual growth, increased physical activity, and better nutrition.

Research consistently demonstrates the benefits of confidence. Whether at work or during leisure activities, confident individuals have a clear advantage. They embrace challenge and work tenaciously to reach their goals. They perform better, feel a greater sense of control over their lives, and experience a heightened sense of well-being.

It's Not Magic

So, how does this work? How do optimism and confidence lead to better health and higher levels of achievement?

The answer to these questions is found, at least partially, in goal setting and how one pursues his or her goals. As noted earlier, individuals who are optimistic expect more good than bad, believing positive results are more plentiful than negative ones. Similarly, confident individuals trust their ability to do what it takes to achieve success; their mantra is "I can do that." Because of these positive beliefs, individuals who are optimistic and confident don't shrink away from challenges. In fact, they intentionally set challenging goals—ones requiring significant effort. The end result is high aspirations that focus effort and drive achievement.

In addition to setting challenging goals, optimistic and confident individuals are relentless in pursuit of their goals. Even when faced with significant obstacles, they are not easily dissuaded.

Positive thinking results in grit, which ultimately leads to better performance and well-being. The connection between a can-do attitude and success isn't magical thinking; rather, these positive patterns of thought empower the individuals who possess them to set challenging goals and then take an active role in reaching them. A feedback loop is established in which each goal achieved adds to a reservoir of optimism and confidence, fueling the next success—and on it goes, creating a positive upward spiral.

Not So Fast

At this point, you might be thinking, "Not so fast! Isn't there a downside to positive thinking? Can't misplaced optimism and unbridled confidence lead to disaster?" Perhaps you have a friend who underestimated the seriousness of an illness and, as a result, failed to seek appropriate medical care. Or you may know a businesswoman whose over-assurance put her organization in jeopardy.

If we take a balanced, honest look at positive thinking, we discover it is not without risk. Misplaced optimism and confidence may cause us to over-invest in goals that are too risky or unobtainable. And, as a result, we waste resources on projects destined to fail. Uncritical positive thinking may cause us to rigidly pursue an ineffective or costly course of action. Because of our unflagging confidence in current strategies, we may be unwilling to change direction, even in the face of compelling evidence suggesting the current approach is taking us in the wrong direction. There is even a risk that positive thinking will actually result in decreased performance. If we are inordinately optimistic, we may become complacent, unwilling to invest the effort necessary to succeed.

To provide the competitive edge we are looking for, optimism and confidence must be grounded in reality. Positive thinking is not a substitute for good judgment and hard work; nor is it wishful thinking or unfounded self-assurance. Sandra Schneider, a leading optimism researcher, summarized this approach to optimism when she wrote: "Realistic optimism relies on regular reality checks to update assessment of progress, fine-tune one's understanding of potential opportunities, refine causal models of situations, and re-evaluate planned next steps."

In my view, the best approach is to be flexible in your use of optimism and confidence. If a goal is unobtainable, too costly, or too risky, then make a course correction—don't waste your positivity on endeavors with a low probability of success. But when a project is worth doing and doable, then by all means expect good outcomes and believe in your ability to get the job done. The goal is to focus your optimism and confidence on outcomes over which you have control. Invest your can-do mindset when your actions have a direct influence on the results. If the resources are available and you have the right skillset, then proceed expecting a good outcome. Choose your course wisely and, once chosen, pursue it with grit fueled by positive thinking.

The Can-do Leader

To this point, I have described the value of a can-do mindset. This section will get down to the nuts and bolts of how we, as leaders, can become more optimistic and confident. Fortunately, a can-do attitude isn't a fixed, immutable trait. It's amenable to change.

The Optimistic Leader

The primary way to nurture optimism is to limit pessimistic thinking while simultaneously learning to think more optimistically. As noted earlier, when faced with a negative occurrence, pessimists automatically begin to think "It's going to last forever," "It's going to undermine everything," and "It's all my fault." Alternatively, optimists focus on the more favorable aspects of a negative experience by being lenient toward the past, actively appreciating the positive aspects of the current situation, and emphasizing possible future opportunities.

How about you? In general, are you a more optimistic person or are you a bit on the pessimistic side? Think back to the last difficult experience you had at work. As you recall this experience, try to remember the thoughts that went through your mind. Did you find yourself automatically thinking, "This is the worst. I'll never recover!"?

Were you a merciless self-critic; willingly throwing yourself under the bus? If so, what was the impact? Did the negativity narrow your focus to all that was wrong in your world and sour your mood?

Or were you more optimistic? Were you lenient with yourself, able to find some good in the difficulty, and remain positive about the future? Could you give yourself a break, accept appropriate personal responsibility and focus on ways to improve performance without self-recrimination? Even in the midst of this difficulty, could you identify some positive aspects of the experience and reframe this problem in the best possible light? If your interpretation was optimistic, what was the impact? Did you remain positive and cope better?

The next time you encounter a setback, I suggest you pay attention to the thoughts that automatically come to mind. If you discover your thoughts are more pessimistic than you would like, actively challenge the negative thoughts and reinterpret the situation in a more positive light. Give yourself a break; be as lenient on yourself as possible. Identify what you did well. Accept appropriate responsibility, but there's no need to be overly self-critical. Make the best possible interpretation of the current difficulty. What did you learn? How can you use what you learned to do better next time? Is there any humor in the situation? Don't let this setback affect your view of the future—remain positive. As you challenge your pessimistic interpretations and substitute more optimistic ones, observe the impact on your feelings and actions.

I recently found myself in the midst of a downward spiral fueled by pessimistic thinking. One beautiful summer morning I planned to begin my day by attending a lecture. Unfortunately, I hit the snooze button a few too many times. It was now unavoidable—I was going to miss it. Immediately, a parade of negative thoughts began marching through my mind "I can't believe I slept so late." "I let myself down." "My day is ruined." As you might imagine, my countenance fell and my mood soured. I experienced a downward emotional cycle, perpetuated by mental negativity. Fortunately, I caught myself, consciously paused, and intentionally began to reinterpret the situation. I focused on the value of this newfound margin in my life. Because I couldn't make the lecture, I now had an extra hour in my day—an unexpected gift. Taking a few deep breaths, I gave myself a break and considered the possibility that I needed to sleep more than I needed to hear a lecture and I would have a better day because it began at a slower pace. This reframing of my experience changed the trajectory of my day. By stopping and redirecting, I initiated a positive, creative, upward spiral.

I wish I could tell you this is always the case for me, but I assure you it is not. I'm sharing this experience with you in order to encourage you to nurture your own optimism. When you experience a setback be lenient with yourself, look for the good in the situation, and remain positive about the future.

The Confident Leader

Confidence, like optimism, is amenable to change. Research suggests that self-assurance primarily comes through mastery, observation, encouragement, and well-being:

Mastery: Success is an effective way to boost confidence. We tend to be most sure of ourselves when we are doing things that we do well. James Maddux, a social scientist who has extensively studied self-efficacy, states it this way: "Our own attempts to control our environments are the most powerful source of self-efficacy information. Successful attempts at control that I attribute to my efforts will strengthen self-efficacy for that behavior domain. Perceptions of failure at control attempts usually diminish self-efficacy." We are more confident when taking on projects requiring a skillset we have mastered. When we believe our actions influence outcomes, we are more likely to act.

If you desire to build confidence in a new area of interest, do what you can to ensure success in that area: set obtainable goals, devise workable plans, and break down complex tasks into small concrete steps that can be easily accomplished. Each step you complete will contribute to your feeling of mastery. Over time, as you reach your goals, you will experience the confidence that is associated with a sense of accomplishment. You will be able to say, "I can do that!"

Observation: Observing others is another source of self-assurance. Confidence often increases when we see others successfully execute actions we desire to master in our own lives. This vicarious learning builds mental expectancies within us regarding what will happen if we pursue a particular course of action.

For others to be effective role models, they must be similar to us, and the tasks they are performing must be like the ones we desire to perform. If the people we observe have more resources, a wider knowledge base, or a different skillset, we tend to discount their example because their situation is too dissimilar. It's hard to relate and, as a result, we don't gain confidence from observing their success. In contrast, if those we desire to emulate are peers, we are more likely to view them as plausible role models and their success will boost our self-assurance. Because their experience is comparable to ours, we assume "If they can do it, I can do it." In addition, for others to set the example, the tasks they perform must be analogous to the tasks we hope to master. The more parallel a task is, the more likely it will boost our confidence.

As I mentioned earlier, my job includes training resident physicians. During residency training, the primary pedagogical method is direct supervision at the bedside. The strength of this approach lies in the learning that occurs when resident doctors watch experienced physicians caring for patients. By observing, residents not only learn the details of what to do, but they also develop an "I can do that" belief. This confidence enables them to practice independently once they have completed their training.

Encouragement: Along with mastery and observation, encouragement is a key source of confidence. We love to hear others say, "You can do it" or "I believe in you." Words of encouragement empower us to try new things and persevere in the face of adversity. For words of encouragement to be meaningful, however, they must come from a source that is credible and genuine, and the words have to be believable:

- If an individual tells us we can do something we clearly have no business even trying, we will automatically dismiss the words as an empty attempt to make us feel better.
- If we don't respect the person offering the encouraging words or he hasn't shown himself to be trustworthy, we won't accept his encouragement at face value.

- If the encourager doesn't appear to mean what she says, or is only trying to make us feel better, then her words will have little value and may even be counterproductive.

Our confidence is enhanced by genuine words of encouragement spoken by individuals we trust.

Jamie, the vice president of information technology for a publicly traded, multinational corporation, traces his confidence to the encouragement he received from his mother and father. His parents actively expressed their care for him and their interest in his life. They consistently told him he could do anything he set his mind to. As an adult, Jamie continues to benefit from the encouragement he received from them. It's a lasting source of confidence in his life, and an important reason for his current success.

Well-being: Confidence has a physical dimension. If we feel physically anxious when approaching a task, it doesn't matter how many times we have successfully completed that particular task, we will approach it with timidity. Conversely, when we feel a sense of peace or calm, we can approach even novel tasks with vigor and determination.

In addition, being physically fit is associated with self-efficacy. When we exercise, eat well, and get enough rest, we experience an overall sense of control and competence. I know this is true for me. When I am active, fill my plate with nutritious foods, and get at least seven hours of sleep (see Chapter 4: *Energy*), I feel more self-assured and approach every dimension of my life with more energy and engagement.

Mastery, observation, encouragement, and well-being are proven sources of confidence. By leveraging these sources, we are able to approach even the most challenging tasks with self-assurance.

Collective Optimism and Confidence

A group with a can-do attitude is capable of extraordinary achievement. When everyone on a team confidently and optimistically pulls in the same direction, a synergy occurs that amplifies the efforts and abilities of each individual team member.

This section describes three approaches to encouraging team optimism and confidence: ensure success, think positively, and encourage others.

Ensure Success

One of the most reliable sources of collective optimism and confidence is success. Nothing does more to build an active, persistently engaged group than positive outcomes. There is a mutual, reciprocal causality in which success and positive thinking build on each other. Today's success is tomorrow's source for optimism and confidence, which then fuels the next day's achievement.

As a leader, when you help the teams you lead achieve their goals, you are contributing to the development of a can-do mindset. The group as a whole begins to believe in itself and expects to do well. The end product is collective grit, success, and well-being.

Think Positively

Along with success, the way a leader interprets events in the life of a team has a major impact on motivation and *esprit de corps*. Success doesn't automatically result in a more optimistic and confident team; nor do setbacks necessarily result in a decrement in optimism and confidence. How a leader frames these experiences helps determine their impact.

A team experiencing success benefits when its leader interprets this success as being linked to effort, likely to continue, and predictive of success in other areas. Even when doing well, team members like hearing messages such as "You really made a difference," and "I can't wait to see what this team will do in the future." These empowering messages link past actions with current success and create anticipation for even greater accomplishments in the future. The result is a team consisting of members who believe in the efficacy of their effort and who expect to continue to do well.

Of equal importance is how leaders interpret negative outcomes. When teams experience setbacks, their leaders can limit the negative impact by being lenient, making the best possible interpretation of what happened, and remaining positive about the future.

Be Lenient About the Past: A team having a difficult time is encouraged by supportive words like, "It happens to everyone," "It's not that bad," and "You can't control everything." By offering these kinds of interpretations, leaders help team members maintain self-esteem and avoid over-personalization.

See Good in the Present: Teams benefit from leaders who look for the positives in negative situations; consistently asking: "Where's the opportunity in this challenge?" There are often hidden blessings, even in the midst of the most disruptive experiences. By identifying these blessings, leaders help maintain the collective optimism and confidence of the teams they lead.

Expect a Bright Future: Leaders can strengthen a team by trusting its ability to rebound from adversity. Teams benefit from leaders who continue to believe in their teams, even when these teams are in the middle of a difficult stretch.

Leaders who make positive interpretations of events augment success and mitigate the negative impact of setbacks. By viewing events from a positive perspective, leaders help the teams they lead develop and maintain a can-do attitude.

Encourage Others

Words of encouragement boost team optimism and confidence. Team members benefit when leaders offer positive feedback that is specific, reality-based, genuine, and spoken in the moment.

Real-Time: If there is too much time between an action and a leader's positive input, the impact is diminished. Encouraging feedback has its greatest impact when it's given contemporaneously with the desired action.

Specific: General comments like "good job" or "way to go" are less efficacious than specific comments like "I appreciate the extra time you spent on the project" or "Your report helped us secure the account."

Believable: For positive feedback to have its desired impact it must be realistic and genuine; otherwise, it's ignored. Compliments that are inaccurate or unearned may even decrease team morale.

Leaders who ensure success, think positively, and encourage others contribute to team optimism and confidence. A collective can-do spirit is an important asset for any organization.

One Leader's Experience

Erica is a communications director for a large, rapidly growing non-profit organization. She leads a team of high-capacity professionals who work under demanding production timelines. There is an ever-present risk her team will become overwhelmed and discouraged.

Below is a description of her approach to a particularly difficult day in the life of her team. As you read this description, observe how she uses past successes to build the team's confidence and optimism. Also, note her use of humor to cope with stress, strengthen connections, and build a positive emotional climate.

Our communications team was having a rough day. All five of us felt overwhelmed and tired. The requests were piling in and we walked into our morning team meeting a bit zoned out. I named the chaos and challenged the team to rise above it. Together, we looked at a couple of recent projects we did well. We talked about the good in each process and discussed how we overcame challenges to get each project done. By the end of the meeting we felt more cohesive and encouraged.

When I got back to my office it occurred to me that I could actually take control and lead with positivity. I had the power to change a few factors in an effort to foster a positive emotional climate. I decided that we don't laugh enough as a team, and it's on me to lead that effort. So I decided I'd do something fun in the afternoon to lift spirits.

Around 3 p.m. that day, I stormed into the design office and said "Liz! Why aren't you on Twitter?!"

Liz is our newest designer, who is so deeply talented that at times she wants to shut out the rest of the world to focus on her art—which is great, except the rest of our team talks on Twitter throughout the day. Liz recently told me she was feeling a greater need for relational connection with our team. Twitter would be a simple fix for that. In the past she has expressed a fear of social media. I was determined to help her overcome that fear. And I was going to use it to laugh and lift our team spirit.

Liz replied, "Well I don't know much about it." I said, "That's okay, we will teach you. We want to talk to you on there once in a while! Okay team, if we can get Liz on Twitter and have her use it to engage in conversation one time, then I will bring donuts in tomorrow morning!"

They laughed.

Ten minutes later Liz followed me on Twitter and began talking to our team online. Her anxiety and reservations faded and she was all smiles. She felt included and valued, and I was happy that our team was laughing once again. Other staff members were also congratulating her on her new Twitter presence. She was beaming with pride.

Oh, and of course they all enjoyed the donuts the next morning.

An Experiment

In this chapter, I have suggested we are not mindless automatons victimized by circumstances. Rather, we are thinking beings who mentally process and interpret everything going on around us. As a result, our thoughts, perceptions, interpretations, and beliefs have a significant impact on how our lives turn out.

Below are some suggestions designed to help you and those you lead develop a can-do mindset. After implementing these suggestions for a few days, observe their impact. Do you approach your day thinking, "Yes, I can do this!"? Are you bringing more positivity and energy to your daily activities? And what about those you lead? Are they more engaged? Do optimism and confidence affect how they approach the challenges in their day?

The Can-do Leader:

- Optimism
  - *Be Lenient About the Past*: Be your own best friend. The next time you experience a setback, learn from it and move on. Don't be overly negativistic or self-critical. Remain positive.
  - *Look for Good in the Present*: At the end of each day, ask yourself the question: "What is good in my life right now?"
  - *Expect a Better Future*: Trust that your efforts will pay off. Believe you will reach your goals.

- Confidence
  - *Mastery*: Spend time each day doing at least one activity you do well. Play life to your strengths.
  - *Observation*: Find a role model or mentor who makes you better at the tasks you most enjoy—observe and learn.
  - *Encouragement*: Spend time each day with positive people who believe in you.
  - *Well-being*: Engage in activities that contribute to your health and well-being. Eat well, exercise often, and get the rest you need.

The Can-do Team:

- *Ensure Success*: Ask team members how you can help them meet their objectives.
- *Think Positive*: If your team is currently struggling, be lenient, look for the good, and expect future success. If your team is experiencing success, make the connection between effort and positive outcome and predict that the current success is likely to continue.
- *Encourage Others*: Identify specific ways to encourage team members. Point out what they are doing well.

KEY CONCEPTS

Thoughts influence how our lives turn out

The way we think has a major impact on our feelings and actions. While there are certainly many aspects of life beyond our control, we are not solely victims of our environment. By expecting the best and trusting in our capacity to make a difference, we can select a path that leads to success and well-being. Our minds give us the capacity to choose the life we desire.

Positive thinking works through grit

When we expect a good outcome and believe in our ability to effect change, we are more likely to be active and persistent problem solvers; there is no obstacle too big to overcome. Positive beliefs result in dogged determination.

C
O
M eaning & Passion
E
U
P

THREE

Meaning & Passion

A Life Worth Living

Everyone has his own specific vocation or mission in life; everyone must carry out a concrete assignment that demands fulfillment. Therein he cannot be replaced, nor can his life be repeated. Thus, everyone's task is unique as his specific opportunity to implement it.

—Viktor Frankl

What if you had never been born?

The classic movie *It's a Wonderful Life* tells the story of George Bailey (James Stewart). George grew up in the small town of Bedford Falls, where his father and uncle had founded a building and loan—a business his father hoped George would someday run. George's vision for his life, however, went far beyond the borders of his hometown. He dreamed of traveling the world, going to college, becoming rich, and building airfields, skyscrapers, and bridges. George could not imagine, under any circumstance, that he would remain in the community where he had grown up. "If I don't get away, I will bust," he once exclaimed. In his mind, Bedford Falls was a crummy little town—no place for anyone who wanted to do anything of significance.

However, not everything turned out as George had planned. Through a series of unfortunate and ill-timed events, his dreams never materialized. On the very day he was packing to travel abroad and then go to college, his father died. Without his father's leadership, the building and loan was sure to be acquired by its competitor, so George postponed his departure. On his wedding day, when George and his bride, Mary (Donna Reed), were leaving town for their honeymoon, there was a run on the building and loan. A large number of depositors wanted to cash out their accounts, but there wasn't enough in reserve. With no other resources, the newlyweds gave the money they had planned to use for their honeymoon to cover the shortfall.

At every turn, George's attempts to pursue his dreams were frustrated. He was hopelessly tied to a small town, with no plausible exit strategy.

One snowy Christmas Eve, an $8,000 deposit was lost, and George's world completely fell apart. He feared he would be accused of embezzlement, the building and loan would fail, and he would go to jail. What he had spent his entire adult life working to preserve would be erased in an instant. This event precipitated a crisis from which he saw no means of escape. Believing he had completely wasted his life, he ran onto a bridge spanning an icy river, intending to jump.

Hearing about the lost deposit and George's desperate situation, his family and friends began to pray. Those who had been helped over the years by his sacrifice and kindness were asking God to intervene. They prayed because, although he never travelled, went to college, or built skyscrapers, George had touched many lives. When his younger brother was nine, he had fallen into an icy pond and George jumped in, saving his life. As a child, George worked in a drugstore. One day, the druggist inadvertently filled some capsules with poison. George discovered the error and refused to deliver them. He had also influenced the lives of scores of individuals through the building and loan, often lending money to lower middle-class working families, enabling them to buy their own homes. His life had made a significant difference in the lives of many, and now those he had influenced were praying on his behalf.

In response, God sent an angel, Clarence (Henry Travers), to intervene. Clarence arrived just in time to save George and hear him exclaim in anguish, "I wish I had never been born." In an effort to help him see the value in his life, Clarence showed George what life in Bedford Falls would have been like if, indeed, he had never existed. Without George, his brother died because no one was there to jump into the pond and save him. The druggist spent time in prison for poisoning a child. None of the homes or businesses funded by the building and loan were built. George's life and his many acts of kindness had a profound impact on others, prompting Clarence to observe, "Strange isn't it? Each man's life touches so many other lives, when he isn't around he leaves an awful hole, doesn't he?"

After seeing the meaningful impact he had had on others, George experienced a change of heart. He began begging for his life back. Hearing his plea, God returned everything back to the way it had been, and, overjoyed, George immediately ran home to see his family. He arrived to find the police waiting to arrest him for misappropriating funds, but just as they were issuing a warrant for his arrest, his wife arrived with many of George's friends. In addition to praying for him, they were gathering donations to replace the $8,000 that had been lost. Though not individually wealthy, these friends and family members donated what they could and easily paid the debt.

George Bailey lived a meaningful life—one that made a very real difference. And in fact, his story is an inspiring reminder of our own value. Each of us is born with a life worth living—a calling that, if unheeded, will leave a hole no one else can fill.

The Intersection of Meaning and Passion

As illustrated by the fictional George Bailey, everyone has something to offer. The success of any group is dependent upon each person making a contribution. Only by inspiring grit in individuals at every level is it possible for an organization to reach its full potential.

In this chapter, I propose that the kind of wholehearted, persistent investment that results in high-level success is found at the intersection of meaning and passion. Long-term commitment that brings out the very best in us is motivated by what we value (meaning) and what we love (passion).

Amy Wrzesniewski, a faculty member at the Yale School of Management and an expert in finding meaning in our employment, suggests that we can view work from three perspectives—as a job, career, or calling:

- Individuals who approach what they do as a job think of work primarily as a means for earning income. Work is a simple work-for-pay transaction. The employee puts in the time and the employer signs the paychecks.
- Work can also be viewed as a career. From this perspective, the current job is viewed as a stepping-stone to the next. The goal is to climb the corporate ladder and to one day have a desk in the corner office.
- Some consider their employment a calling. They are passionate about what they do and find it meaningful. It's part of their self-esteem and identity.

Wrzesniewski proposes that "a calling is assumed to be unique to the person, comprising activities individuals believe they must do to fulfill their unique purpose in life, and offers a path to connect with one's true self." Individuals who desire to fulfill their calling focus on making a contribution to others and serving a greater good. Their primary motivation is the pursuit of an important value rather than a paycheck or the next position on the org chart.

Employees who view what they do as a calling are more satisfied with both their work and their lives in general. They spend more time at their place of employment and are more persistent when pursuing difficult challenges. As a result, they outperform their peers.

Finding value in one's activities is a key to grit, and regardless of the role or task, an organization's success is fundamentally dependent upon individuals finding meaning in what they do. Take, for example, call-center employees who perform the notoriously difficult task of soliciting funds. Not only is their work highly monotonous, but they also experience frequent rejection—and sometimes open hostility. As a result, these employees typically have difficulty maintaining motivation, and their turnover rate is high.

Adam Grant, the author of *Give and Take*, studied the persistence and performance of callers who were soliciting scholarship donations from university alumni. In this study, he found that fundraisers who met with a student who had benefited from their fundraising efforts spent more time speaking with donors and raised more money than the fundraisers who did not meet a beneficiary. In fact, the callers who had briefly talked with a scholarship recipient spent 142 percent more time soliciting funds and raised 171 percent more revenue! Armed with tangible evidence of the positive impact of their efforts, these call-center employees were more persistent and successful. Simply meeting an individual whose life was improved by their efforts gave them a reason to dial the next number.

We, too, invest in what we value (meaning) and what we love (passion). Grit is motivated by our personal beliefs regarding what is worth doing and what is enjoyable and interesting. When motivated by what matters most, we will work hard even in the absence of external incentives—and persist even when others are not watching.

Meaning—Do What You Value

... being human always points, and is directed, to something, or someone, other than oneself—be it a meaning to fulfill or another human being to encounter. The more one forgets himself—by giving himself to a cause to serve or another person to love—the more human he is and the more he actualizes himself.

—Viktor Frankl

He was prisoner number 119104.

Born in Vienna, Austria, in 1905, Viktor Frankl became one of the most influential psychiatrists of the 20th century. Over the course of his career, he was professor of neurology and psychiatry at the University of Vienna Medical School, as well as a visiting professor at Harvard University, University of Pittsburg, U.S. International University, and University of Dallas. During his lifetime, he travelled to five continents, lectured at 209 universities and was awarded 29 honorary doctorates from universities all over the world. He also published 39 books. At the time of his death in 1997, his book *Man's Search for Meaning* had been translated into 24 languages and had sold more than 10 million copies. A survey conducted by the Library of Congress and the Book-of-the-Month Club ranked *Man's Search for Meaning* among the 10 most influential books in America.

Frankl was the middle child in a pious Jewish family with three children. During his adolescence, he became fascinated with philosophy and psychiatry, reading most anything he could get his hands on. In high school, he began corresponding with, arguably, Vienna's most famous resident—the internationally renowned founder of psychoanalysis, Sigmund Freud. At age 17, Frankl sent Freud a paper he had written for one of his high school classes. Freud was so favorably impressed by this young student's thoughts and writing he submitted the paper, on Frankl's behalf, to the *International Journal of Psychoanalysis*. In the fall of 1924, Frankl began medical school at the University of Vienna where, in addition to excelling in the classroom, he continued to write and publish articles. After completing his residency, he began practicing psychiatry, eventually becoming chief of neurology at Rothschild Hospital in Vienna.

He was a rising star with a growing national and international reputation. In another time and place, Frankl could have had a storybook life and enviable career; but there was a dark cloud gathering over Vienna and all of Europe.

As Frankl was studying medicine and beginning his professional career, Adolf Hitler's influence was growing and anti-Semitism was on the rise. Jews were experiencing such increasingly brazen and ruthless persecution that even his patients would insult him, calling him a "dirty Jewish swine." In September of 1942, Frankl and his family were arrested and imprisoned in the concentration camp at Theresienstadt. When he and his fellow prisoners arrived at the camp, those who were not immediately sent to the gas chambers were stripped, their possessions were confiscated, and every hair was shaved from their body.

Over the next three years, Frankl was herded from camp to camp and exposed to the most inhumane treatment—the unimaginable had become reality. He and his fellow prisoners were starved, beaten, and forced to labor with grossly inadequate tools and only minimal protection from the elements. When Frankl was liberated in April of 1945, he was severely malnourished, weighing only 83 pounds and suffering from an irregular heart rhythm, edema, and frostbite.

In the midst of one of the darkest periods of human history and the worst possible personal circumstances, Frankl not only survived but, remarkably, developed an optimistic view of the human condition based on what he later described as "an unconditional faith in life's unconditional meaning." The Nazis had taken everything from him except the last of human freedoms, the freedom to choose how he would respond. He observed firsthand, on a daily basis, that a reason to live was essential to survival. Frankl discovered that those who had a person they hoped to see again or a calling they hoped to fulfill would cling to life regardless of the odds. In contrast, those who lost hope would lie on their bunk and no amount of coaxing could persuade them to continue on. Based on his experiences in the concentration camps, Frankl concluded: "There is nothing in the world, I venture to say, that would so effectively help one to survive even the worst conditions as the knowledge that there is meaning in one's life."

During his confinement, Frankl used his expertise as a psychiatrist to help other prisoners make it through the day. In *Man's Search for Meaning*, he describes his encounter with two men who had lost all hope and were on the verge of suicide. In his conversations with them, he helped them find meaning—a reason to live. For one, it was a child he adored who was waiting for him to return. For the other, there was a series of books he wanted to write. Frankl himself found meaning in the hope of seeing his wife again, lecturing about the psychological lessons learned from concentration camps, and finishing a manuscript he had begun. He observed, "A man who becomes conscious of the responsibility he bears toward a human being who affectionately waits for him, or to an unfinished work, will never be able to throw away his life."

To the Nazis, Frankl was nothing more than prisoner number 119104. They did everything they could to reduce his existence to six digits sewn on his shirt. They treated him like a beast to be used up and thrown away. They had mercilessly and with callous disregard taken everything from him, yet he transcended his situation, finding a reason to live in the midst of senseless, abusive mistreatment. Sustained by meaning, he survived to become one of the 20th century's most influential psychiatrists and inspirational writers.

As Frankl's remarkable life so clearly demonstrates, individuals who find meaning, a reason to live, are often able to transcend even the most difficult and horrific of circumstances. Though not a panacea, and the sobering reality is that many died in the concentration camps despite an equally heroic resolve, those who succeed in discovering their unique purpose are often able to overcome and, remarkably, flourish regardless of the circumstances in which they find themselves. Individuals who arrange their lives around what they value are irrepressible—an irresistible force in the relentless pursuit of a dream. The loss of a job, the meltdown of a significant relationship, physical abuse, and financial stress may create angst, detours, and profound heartache; but individuals who have discovered their purpose somehow find the courage to keep moving forward. As with Frankl, meaning transcends the moment and creates the passionate pursuit of a calling that must be fulfilled.

The search for personal meaning involves the identification and pursuit of what one values most. It often, if not exclusively, entails developing an outward focus. It's not found solely in satisfying one's own needs or pursuing personal interests; rather, it's discovered by focusing on making a difference in the lives of others and contributing to the greater good. Meaning is drawn from a cause to embrace, a person to love, a mission to live, or a creative work to complete.

Each of us has a meaning to uncover and pursue—a unique calling. There are commitments only you can make and goals only you can achieve. Your actions in pursuit of this calling become the footprint you leave on this planet—your legacy.

Legacy building may be as simple as the smile you offer to the barista at Starbucks or the helping hand you lend to the person in the next cubicle. Perhaps it's the violin recital you attend to encourage your son or the homework assistance you offer your daughter. Maybe for you it is the business you were destined to start or the team you are best qualified to lead. While there are others who can smile, help, and lead, no one does these things exactly like you and no one occupies the unique position you occupy. Meaning is found by living the life only you can live, making the difference only you can make, and caring for those only you can care for. As George Bailey discovered, your unique calling consists of what the world would miss had you never been born.

Meaning is a powerful, stabilizing force in our individual lives and in society as a whole. If we base our decisions and actions on moment-to-moment feelings or highly variable situational factors, rather than deeply engrained values, we are less persistent and focused. If our primary ambition is immediate gratification, we will change course at the first sign of difficulty. If our only goal is to seek pleasure and avoid pain, then unpleasantness is interpreted as a sign that we are headed in the wrong direction.

In contrast, meaning is highly stable over time. It's largely unaffected by transient feelings or situational variables. If we find deep and lasting value in our families, we will do most anything to assure the stability and longevity of these relationships. Even when we don't feel like it or are busy with other obligations, we will find time to be with those we care about. Similarly, at work, our commitment keeps us motivated even when there are many barriers to success. On any given day, we may not feel like doing our job; yet, because of our dedication to co-workers and to our organization, we get out of bed and make the commute. Our deeply held values, the ones in which we find meaning, set our direction, stabilize our course, and keep us focused on our calling.

The pursuit of what matters most often requires sacrifice and determination. As a general rule, meaning is not readily found by travelling the path of least resistance. It takes persistent investment to honor one's commitments and achieve one's goals. Without grit no one would write a novel or compose a concerto. Apple, Twitter, and Marriott would not exist without visionaries who were willing to invest the sweat equity necessary to ensure success.

Interestingly, there is a paradox associated with the search for meaning. As individuals focus on the welfare of others and contribute to a cause bigger than themselves, they often benefit as much, or more, than the people they are trying to help. In his book *Give and Take*, Adam Grant highlights this paradox. He concludes that givers do better than takers. Over time, those who give without concerning themselves with what they will receive in return (givers) do better than those who focus on what they are able to get from others (takers). Seeking meaning, though other-focused, is not purely altruistic. Grant notes that givers build better networks, are more successful, are more receptive to feedback, work harder, are more persistent, and make those around them better. He also notes givers are at the top of their class in medical school, the most productive engineers, and the top salespeople.

This paradox is central to Frankl's worldview. He observed: "For success, like happiness, cannot be pursued; it must ensue, and it only does so as the unintended side-effect of one's personal dedication to a cause greater than oneself or as the by-product of one's surrender to a person other than oneself."

Martin Seligman has developed an exercise designed to demonstrate that "an orientation to the welfare of others is, in the long run, more satisfying than an orientation to one's own pleasure." In this exercise, which Seligman calls *Fun Versus Philanthropy*, participants are asked to engage in an activity they find highly enjoyable. This activity can be anything they find pleasurable—like eating a fine meal, spending time with good friends, or watching their favorite television show. Then, they are encouraged to spend an equal amount of time doing something focused on contributing to the welfare of others. This philanthropic act can be anything that benefits another person. Predictably, individuals who try this exercise find pleasure in the fun activities. What may be less intuitive is that philanthropy is also associated with positive feelings—and, interestingly, the positivity associated with helping others lasts longer than the positivity associated with seeking pleasure.

You may wish to try this exercise for yourself. Sometime in the next few days, spend time engaging in a fun activity and then spend an equal amount of time doing something philanthropic. Begin by engaging in an activity exclusively because it feels good. Select anything you find enjoyable. Then, switch your focus and spend time helping another person. You may tutor a student, assist a colleague with a difficult project, or help your neighbor move some furniture. The particular activity you choose is not what's important. What's important is that you do something to benefit another person without expecting anything in return. After you have completed this exercise, consider its effect on you. Do you agree with Seligman's observation that an orientation to the welfare of others is more satisfying than an orientation to your own pleasure?

Meaning gives direction and purpose to our lives. It's our "why"—our reason for getting out of bed in the morning. When we have identified our unique calling, we are able to overcome the difficulties we encounter and, with grit, pursue our commitments and goals.

Passion—Do What You Love

Passion is what we are most deeply curious about, most hungry for, will most hate to lose in life. It is the most desperate wish we need to yell down the well in our lives. It is whatever we pursue merely for its own sake, what we study when there are no tests to take, what we create though no one may ever see it.

It makes us forget that the sun rose and set, that we have bodily functions, and personal relations that could use a little tending.

—Gregg Levoy

David hit the career lottery. He absolutely loves his job. But unlike the lottery, his success is not based on a number drawn at random; rather it is a result of the intentional pursuit of his passion. For as long as I have known him, he has been a complete computer geek. From a very young age, he displayed a knack for understanding technology, creating applications for handheld devices, and, most importantly, responding to my requests for free help when I had a vexing computer problem.

After receiving a degree in electrical engineering, David began developing software for a wide array of applications in a variety of industries. Currently, though living in Indianapolis, he is a project manager and software developer for a highly successful equity firm in California. When I asked him why a West Coast company would hire him and allow him to work from his home in the Midwest, he stated it was based on his ability to adapt to customer needs, his problem-solving capacity, and his can-do attitude. He manages projects well and meets demanding production schedules. Both he and his company benefit because he is doing what he loves and what he does best.

We all have a natural affinity for certain activities. We are simply drawn to them. These are our passions. They are as unique as our fingerprints—one person's drudgery is another's delight. Some people love to hike, while others spend their day with a book in their hand. Some dig into the details with great vigor, while others find joy in the big picture. For David, though he may not know exactly why, writing software has piqued his interest. Don't tell his employer, but he might very well do the job for less money because it brings him such great satisfaction.

Our passions are the things we love—the parts of life we connect with emotionally. Sometimes our response is jubilant, expressed in ecstatic outbursts like the crowd leaving the stands, rushing the field, and tearing down the goalposts after a last-minute touchdown. Or the senior management team shouting and exchanging high-fives after securing a major account. More commonly, though, passions are experienced and expressed more subtly. For those who love nature, the feeling of awe associated with ascending a mountain peak may be so understated it is barely noticeable. At work, the satisfaction of finishing an interesting project is the silent reward for a job well done.

Perhaps because of the associated positivity, our passions motivate us, influencing the path we choose in life and the activities in which we engage. We tend to be intensely driven to seek that which captures our imagination—the things we do for their own sake. Our interests compel us to read late into the night, disregarding our need for sleep. It's why we stay past quitting time even when there is no imminent deadline. Success in any field is difficult to imagine without some level of interest and curiosity. Where there is passion, there is grit.

Frankl's inspirational journey of survival, resilience, and transcendence was sustained by his relentless search for meaning. Who could ever have guessed the desire to publish a manuscript would enable him to resist the focused hatred of a nation bent on his destruction? The backstory of David's success is his focused passion. He invests and feels a deep sense of personal satisfaction because he is succeeding at what he loves. Meaning and passion drive commitment, ultimately helping individuals find their unique calling and reach their potential.

Live at the Intersection of Meaning and Passion

To make this more applicable and to help you get a better sense of what you find meaningful and what you are passionate about, consider taking a few minutes at the end of your day to engage in the following exercise:

Begin by envisioning your *best possible self*. "Imagine yourself in the future, after everything has gone as well as it possibly could. You have worked hard and succeeded at accomplishing all your life goals. Think of this as a realization of your life dreams, and of your own best potentials." In this imagined future …

- What are things like in your significant relationships?
- What have you achieved at work?
- Is there a cause you have made your own?

- What is the place of spirituality in your day?
- How are you spending your leisure time?

Then, organize your thoughts and describe this imagined best self in writing. Compose a brief description of your ideal future.

Now, with your best possible self in mind, review the activities you engaged in over the past 24 hours. Did your actions today move you one step closer to a better tomorrow? Did you work hard and persist at tasks designed to build the future you desire?

Next, imagine what the *best possible day* might look like for you—one fully invested in meaningful and interesting pursuits. Consider what you would need to change in order to create a better future for yourself. What activities would you need to add? What would you need to stop doing?

To further clarify and refine your thinking, repeat this exercise on each of the next few days. Begin by reviewing and revising the written description you created of your best possible self. Refine your description so it more closely represents what you value (meaning) and love (passion). Then review your day focusing on the questions: Am I currently investing in activities that will help me reach valued goals? And, do my actions bring out the very best in me?

Finally, plan the next day so its focus centers on using more time and energy in pursuit of what matters most to you, living as much as possible at the intersection of meaning and passion.

The purpose of this exercise is to help you identify more clearly the commitments you hold most dear. This is your bucket list of valued goals—the life you would be living if your dreams were to be fully realized.

Lead at the Intersection of Meaning and Passion

Simon Sinek, the author of *Start With Why*, begins his popular TED talk with the question: "How do you explain when things don't go as we assume—or, better, how do you explain when others are able to achieve things that seem to defy all of the assumptions?" In the remainder of his talk, he proposes an answer to this question, suggesting that high-level success, success that defies the assumptions, is inspired by visionary leaders who have a clearly defined *why*. As an example, Sinek points to the Wright Brothers who were able to succeed at powered, manned flight before anyone else because of their relentless pursuit of a singular objective. They were not the best funded or the most academically prepared to be first, but their laser-focused passion inspired a steeled determination that empowered them to outperform others. Driven by a single-minded focus, they made history.

Individuals and teams achieve the most when they have a compelling why—a set of deeply held core values (meaning) and interests (passion) that guide and motivate them. In this section, I propose that leaders inspire the kind of determination demonstrated by the Wright Brothers when they define what's important, set the example, and create a narrative.

Define What's Important

Every team has its own values. These are non-negotiable core beliefs. They are fundamental commitments believed to be universally good—the right things to pursue regardless of the situation. Individuals who endorse a particular team's values are considered part of the in-group.

A team's core values may include …

- Service
- Benevolence
- Profitability
- Integrity
- Grit
- Honesty
- Independence
- Loyalty
- Kindness
- Care
- Spirituality
- Comfort
- Excitement
- Equality
- Freedom
- Happiness
- Pleasure
- Beauty
- Friendship
- Gratitude
- Autonomy
- Achievement
- Benevolence
- Power

Take a minute to identify the important commitments endorsed by the teams you lead. Review them with the following questions in mind:

- Are the values expressed in actions?
- Is there a basic congruence between what the team views as important and how time and resources are used?
- Are certain values consistently supported and others ignored?

If a particular team you lead doesn't have clearly articulated values, consider the following exercise. Get your team members together and ask them …

- What teams do you most admire? Why?
- What is it about any team that makes it inherently good and should be considered good by all teams in all situations?
- Regarding our team, what is it about us that is most admirable?
- Are there any important values our team is missing?

After having a conversation using similar questions, one not-for-profit organization identified two important values: humility and hunger. Its leaders aspire to attract employees who share these fundamental commitments. They look for team members with a fierce professional resolve and a can-do attitude. Yet, they don't want this hunger to be diminished by arrogance. They hire people who are more concerned about progress than who gets the credit. Humility and hunger have served this organization well. There's a positive climate in the workplace and high-level achievement is the norm.

For fun, apply the above exercise to your family. Get everyone together and ask them …

- What families do you most admire? Why?
- What is it about any family that makes it inherently good and should be considered good by all families in all situations?
- Regarding our family, what is it about us that is most admirable?
- Are there any important values our family is missing?

Two values my wife and I communicated to our children were "have fun" and "cooperate." We desired for our children to enjoy themselves. Yet we hoped they would do so without being disruptive or having to be the center of attention. Whether they were at school, on the sports field, or in a friend's home, our desire was for them to smile and laugh often while getting along well with others.

A leader's capacity to identify and communicate values is fundamental to any organization's success. When every team member is invested in what's important, a synergy of effort is created, which brings out the best in everyone involved.

Set the Example

Meaning and passion develop in the context of our interactions with others. They aren't acquired in isolation; rather, they emerge and are endorsed within families, teams, organizations, and cultures. Actions and interests that are affirmed tend to become part of the collective ethos, whereas those that are censured are discarded.

What we value and what we love develop, in part, by observing others. We emulate the people we hold in high esteem. For example, I attribute my work ethic and compassion to my parents. You could set your watch by my dad's schedule. He was at work by 7 each morning and at home by 5:30 each evening. In addition, when he wasn't at his day job, he was working on projects on our 80-acre farm. Likewise, my mother invested her energies in cooking, cleaning, and nurturing her eight children. And, as if this weren't enough, she had another full-time job attending nearly all of our sporting events and school programs.

Along with hard work, my parents consistently looked outside of themselves. They were always ready to assist anyone in need. Our home had a revolving door with a steady stream of visitors. There was often an extra place set at our dining room table to feed a friend who, mysteriously, dropped by at mealtime. Many in my hometown were the recipients of Mom and Dad's gracious hospitality.

While my work ethic and compassion originated from my parents, Tom Ewald, my psychology professor in college, inspired my love for learning and interest in psychology and medicine. Tom is a tall, balding man with an amazing intellect. When asked a question, he pauses, nods his head slightly, furrows his brow and offers insightful and thought-provoking responses. As a young college student, I remember thinking that someday I would like to have his insight into the human condition. His example has shaped my career.

I find meaning in hard work and compassion, and I love learning and teaching because of the influence of significant people in my life. Without their influence, I would have developed different values and passions.

Like Tom and my parents, Ken Gwirtz leads by example. He is a highly effective leader for one of America's largest medical schools. Over the years, he has chaired scores of committees and held numerous prestigious administrative positions. He is widely respected by students, resident physicians, colleagues, and administrators.

Some of his greatest assets, as a leader, are his integrity and authenticity. His actions are consistent with his values. In particular, he values teaching and providing high quality medical care. Guided by these fundamental commitments, he arrives at work early and is one of the last to leave. He is an active and innovative clinician who is highly invested in patient care. His knowledge and clinical acumen set a high standard of clinical excellence. Colleagues regularly seek his expert advice. Along with his dedication to patient care, Gwirtz is committed to the educational mission of the medical school. He has received numerous teaching awards and mentored countless physicians who look to him as a role model.

Gwirtz's pursuit of excellence influences all who know him. Inspired by his example, the physicians in his department work hard, teach with distinction, and provide high-quality patient care. The integrity with which he pursues meaningful ends brings out the very best in others. His authentic pursuit of what matters most sets a standard and motivates others to follow his lead. His colleagues are better doctors and faculty members because of the high standards he embodies. These standards have become the norm. Teaching excellence and high-quality medical care are the values that permeate everything that is done. These core commitments guide new initiatives and new hires, creating a positive upward cycle. The individuals he leads are more engaged and the university is a better place because of his tireless pursuit of what matters most.

Teams take on the characteristics of their leaders. If a leader wants her team to provide high-quality customer service, then she must be the first to do so. If loyalty is valued, it must come from the top. Leaders communicate what's important by what they do. If a picture is worth a 1,000 words, an example is worth 10,000.

Create a Narrative

We look for meaning in what we do. It's part of our nature to want our actions to matter. There is an inborn desire to look beyond ourselves and make our work, our communities, and our world better places.

Yet it isn't always easy to find meaning. Some work is poorly compensated and certain roles are associated with limited prestige. In fact, there are a number of tasks that are downright nasty. Individuals who hold low-status jobs may have difficulty finding meaning in their work and even more difficulty finding anything to be passionate about. Even in high-status positions, there are often parts of the day that are real turnoffs.

When individuals are unable to find meaning in their work, there is a precipitous drop in effort. If the only incentive is imposed from the outside, at the first sign of difficulty an individual will abandon what he or she is doing and look for something more meaningful and interesting to do. External motivation is much less effective than internal motivation. If one's primary reason for going to work each day is a paycheck, to keep the parents happy, or fulfill someone else's vision, there is little reason to show up or make an effort.

With few exceptions, however, all work has value. Meaning is about the narrative. It is how people mentally frame what they do; not the details of how they spend their time. Finding meaning and passion is an interpretive process—a process of making a connection between what one is doing and why one is doing it. Even jobs that are considered by many to be menial or dirty can be imbued with meaning. Wrzesniewski and her colleagues interviewed a housekeeper in a hospital whose job it was to clean up vomit and excrement on an oncology ward. While most would find this job meaningless, this housekeeper did not. She viewed her work as a calling. She stated:

My job is equally important to the physician. I help these people feel human. At their lowest and most vulnerable point, I help them maintain their dignity. I make it okay to feel awful, to lose control, and to be unable to manage themselves. My role is crucial to the healing process.

Clearly, the meaning of a particular job is not determined by the tasks it entails or its social status; rather its meaning arises from one's beliefs regarding what's important.

A very concrete way leaders help others find meaning in work is by a willingness to do most any task, especially those tasks no one wants to do. When leaders take on an undesirable assignment, they communicate with their actions that a particular role, regardless of its perceived status, has value and is worth doing. For example, Gwirtz is the first to take on the most challenging projects. He often assigns himself difficult tasks, knowing others might lose their motivation if they perceive they are assigned too often to the least desirable jobs. He could use his position to insulate himself from the dirty work. Yet, in his mind, nothing is beneath him. As a result of his example, other employees are more willing to look beyond their own immediate needs and see value in any activity.

Individuals and teams who find meaning in what they do are relentless. They are single-minded in pursuit of what matters most. Like Frankl, those who know their "why" will endure most anything and do most anything to not only survive, but to thrive. Like David, those who find their passion are virtually unstoppable. Like Gwirtz, those who model the pursuit of core values bring out the very best in others.

One Leader's Experience

I asked a highly effective leader to reflect on the concepts covered in this chapter. In particular, I was curious regarding his thoughts on two questions: (1) In your work, what do you find most meaningful and what are you most passionate about? and (2) How do you help those you lead find meaning and passion in their work? The following was his response:

I don't even have to think hard about the first question. By far and away, the part of my job I find most meaningful and am most passionate about is helping. Not winning, but helping. Sometimes that means helping clients solve a real-world problem, sometimes it means helping my colleagues find an answer to an intellectual puzzle, and sometimes it means helping peers develop their strengths. My very best day is when I am able to help someone else succeed publicly (while I am able to remain in the shadows personally).

In response to the second question, the only way to help others find meaning and passion in their work is by finding out where they find meaning and passion in their lives, which means taking the time to get to know them as people. Most people crave being truly known, and it brings me pleasure to learn (and remember) things about people they wish others knew. Once I know someone and discover what lights his fire, the next step is for me to demonstrate that I am genuinely interested in helping him achieve his goals. There are a variety of ways to do this, whether by looking for opportunities that fit his specific strengths (which may mean passing up those opportunities for myself), introducing him to people who share similar interests, recommending books or other resources that will enable him to build on his strengths, or making sure to celebrate his successes in a public way.

The unstated part of this second question is "How do you help those you lead find meaning and passion in those portions of their work they do not find meaningful and are not passionate about?" Sometimes the answer is by speaking the truth in love and telling them that this is not the right career or place for them and encouraging them to explore other opportunities for which they are a better fit. Sometimes the answer is to encourage them to take control of their own career by "stop doing" those things they find to be drudgery and figuring out a way to spend more of their time doing what they love (I'm a big fan of "stop doing" lists.). Sometimes the answer is to help them (and myself) see that even the things that seem to be drudgery can be meaningful if you step back and consider the larger picture.

An Experiment

Consider this experiment.

Intentionally add meaningful and interesting activities to your day. These need not be monumental changes to your routine. Simply spend a bit more time doing things you value and are passionate about. Then, as you make these changes, consider the following questions:

- Are you more persistent and invested when engaged in activities that are related to your values and passions?
- Do you achieve more when pursuing what you find important?
- Do you feel a sense of satisfaction when working on projects that you enjoy and value?

Then, adapt the above experiment to help someone you lead find her calling.

Begin by asking her to describe her *best possible future* and *best possible day* (see above). Then, ask her to adjust the activities of her day so she spends more of her time working to achieve her most treasured goals. As she makes these changes, observe the impact. Does she persist even when faced with significant challenges? Is she more productive? Does she experience a sense of well-being?

KEY CONCEPTS

Everyone matters

You have a calling to fulfill. When you do the things you were put on this planet to do, you thrive and those around you benefit.

Do what matters most

Spend the bulk of your day focusing on what you value and what you love. And, as a leader, help others do the same. Create a climate that encourages those you lead to invest in what matters most—help them live their calling.

COME
Energy
UP

FOUR

Energy

Running on Full

Energy—the sense of being eager to act and capable of action—is a critical, limited, but renewable resource that enables excellence in individuals and organizations. Without effective means for generating and replenishing the energy of individuals in the workplace, no organization can ever be truly great.

—Jane E. Dutton

It's the middle of the afternoon. After attacking my to-do list with vigor for several hours, a subtle change is taking place. I haven't eaten since breakfast. I'm tiring. I'm getting increasingly irritable and finding myself becoming impatient with co-workers. I'm less able to concentrate, and my productivity is declining. I'm starting to disengage. I feel depleted. I'm running on empty.

Energy—without it, we lose focus and our performance suffers; with it, we are engaged and everyone around us benefits. It's fundamentally related to creativity, grit, productivity, and well-being. Employees who are energized by what they do are more committed and satisfied. They also have a greater impact on an organization because their ideas are considered more often and implemented more frequently. When interacting with enthusiastic leaders, team members tend to take more initiative, spend more time working on projects, and invest more of their intellectual capital. In addition, energetic leaders attract high-capacity individuals to their teams. The best performers—like all of us—want to be around leaders who bring excitement to the projects they are working on.

Energy is a complex, multifaceted phenomenon with emotional, mental, and behavioral dimensions:

- *Emotional*: When energized, we experience a sense of vitality. We feel good and approach our day with vigor.
- *Mental*: When mentally alert, we are engaged in the here and now. We are creative, looking for new ways to invest and work beyond what is required.
- *Behavioral*: When excited, we are ready to go the extra mile in order to ensure success. We are active—prepared to do what it takes to reach goals and make a contribution.

Energy is a game changer. It fuels our success. As leaders, one of the challenges we face is how to maintain this essential renewable resource—in ourselves as well as in those whom we lead.

Energy Sources

Every activity we engage in simultaneously adds to and subtracts from our energy. Intuitively, it might be tempting to assume this valuable commodity comes exclusively from rest and relaxation. Common sense would seem to indicate that the best thing we could do to recharge is sit on the couch, flip on the TV, and veg out. But while there's a role for rest, it's only one source of vitality. There are many activities that contribute to a positive energy balance, including the six sources identified below: self-determination, connections, breaks, exercise, nutrition, and sleep.

Self-Determination

Richard Ryan and Edward Deci, from the University of Rochester, propose that we are born with an innate motivation to learn and create. They write: "The fullest representations of humanity show people to be curious, vital, and self-motivated. At their best, they are agentic and inspired, striving to learn; extend themselves; master new skills; and apply their talents responsibly." This proclivity to grow is seen in toddlers who can't seem to get enough sensory input from their environment. These nascent learning machines have a high-motor, self-directed vigor guiding their young lives, wearing out even the most dedicated parent who tries to keep up with their wide-eyed exploration.

However, this innate, self-directed growth isn't immutable. It's susceptible to a variety of influences. It can be encouraged and reinforced, resulting in achievement. Or it can be quenched, resulting in disengagement and apathy.

In particular, our growth is diminished by situations in which our initiatives are met with excessive negativity and multiple roadblocks. When our efforts are criticized, our sense of accomplishment is undermined, and we are prone to withdraw and avoid future challenges. Our innate desire to create is also diminished by settings in which we are micromanaged or extensively controlled by external influences. In an environment offering limited opportunities for autonomy, we lose our desire to contribute. Unnecessary, external control with capricious rules and structures invariably leads to discouragement.

Recently, I was talking with a friend about a chief-of-staff who had invested many years in a large hospital, but who changed jobs because he began to feel his only role was to comply with top-down rules. He was a valued and compassionate leader who had done much to improve the work environment and patient care. But he couldn't continue on in the same role because he had come to believe his primary job product was compliance, as his autonomy was severely limited by a system that was overly rule-bound and protocol driven. So he resigned and found a job allowing more freedom to engage in meaningful activities—one with fewer *got tos* and more *get tos*.

In contrast, our inborn desire to learn and grow is reinforced by environments that foster self-determination. When we do things because we are good at them or because we genuinely want to do them, we experience an automatic energy boost.

There is a phenomenon I have observed, which I call the *Saturday Morning Effect*. It refers to the energy we easily find on days we *get to* determine how we spend our time. We may have had the most horrifically busy workweek, getting up early and staying up late Monday through Friday. On Friday, we may have dragged ourselves to work, gulped our coffee, spent the day hoping no one would see us yawn, and limped home exhausted. Yet, on Saturday morning we are up before dawn and ready to engage in our favorite hobby—fully engaged and energized. What's the difference between Friday and Saturday? Where did all the enthusiasm originate? The answer lies, at least partially, in self-determination. We are invigorated by activities that we freely choose for their own sake.

Take a minute to review the events of the past few days. Were they filled with mostly *get tos* or *got tos*? My guess is that if your time was spent complying with someone else's agenda, little autonomy, and few tasks you would choose because of their inherent meaning, you are likely depleted. However, if you were engaged in projects you found interesting and valuable, ones you authentically chose, I imagine you currently have plenty of energy. Regardless of whether the activities you participated in were at work or at home, if they were to your liking, then, chances are, they made a positive contribution to your level of enthusiasm. Tasks we choose for their own sake fuel our success.

I'm aware it's unrealistic to live without external constraints, requirements, and negative feedback. Life is never 100 percent *get tos*. In fact, I would suggest that most successful individuals have a whole spate of *got tos* in their lives. The goal isn't eliminating all *got tos*; rather, the goal is to include as many *get tos* as possible so we can maintain our investment and persistence.

If you find yourself disengaged and overly fatigued, it may be you are living under the burden of too many imposed, external constraints. The remedy is, when possible, to redesign your day to include more activities of your own choosing—ones that are self-determined rather than other-determined.

Connections

Negative interactions drain energy and decrease momentum. The people around us have a profound impact on our mood and productivity. Even the anticipation of being around an abrasive or negativistic individual will often elicit an immediate, visceral feeling of dread. Our natural bent is to avoid those whose sour demeanor drags us down, because when forced to be around others who rub us the wrong way, our energy level takes a hit. Further, if we are assigned to a team whose members don't get along, that team is likely to significantly underperform.

Conversely, connecting with people we enjoy being around adds fuel to our tank. Jane Dutton, in her book *Energize Your Workplace*, identifies three qualities of work relationships that contribute to vitality: (1) respectful engagement, (2) task enabling, and (3) trusting.

- Respectful engagement consists of communicating verbally and non-verbally to those with whom we interact that they are highly valued and appreciated. It is being fully present in our interactions, not allowing distractions to disrupt our attention and being willing to set ourselves aside in order to understand another person. Others feel respected when we slow our pace, take the time to affirm them, and recognize their accomplishments.
- We energize the workplace by helping others succeed (task enabling). When our colleagues believe we are in their corner, ready to help them accomplish great things, they are often more willing to dream big and work hard to reach their goals.
- Our willingness to trust others builds positive, productive relationships. It involves communicating with our words and actions that we believe those with whom we work will come through.

Work relationships marked by respectful engagement, task enabling, and trusting create enthusiasm and grit.

Spend a few minutes reviewing your most recent conversation with a co-worker. During that encounter, did you respectfully engage, set aside everything, and focus on the person in front of you? Did the interaction enable her to make progress on an important task? Did you communicate your trust, building her confidence? And, finally, was it energizing or depleting?

Breaks

Recently I hired a contractor to replace the roof on my house. Early in the morning, his crew of 11 workers ascended ladders and in one hour removed the old shingles and stripped my roof down to its decking. They worked with energy and focus all morning. At noon they ate lunch, rolled out mats, and napped under a shade tree. Refreshed by this midday break, they returned to the task at hand with renewed vigor. By the end of the workday, I had a new roof.

Paradoxically, stepping back and taking a break will frequently contribute to our capacity to move forward. When we focus too long on a task, we become fatigued and our performance declines. Even when engaging in an activity we genuinely enjoy and greatly value, at some point we will grow weary and our enthusiasm will wane. Sometimes the best way to improve performance is to disengage and take a break. Individuals and teams that know when to step back are more creative and make better decisions.

A break may include a wide variety of activities. It may be a mental distraction—something that takes your mind off the task at hand, like a conversation at the water cooler. You may simply put your feet up, close your eyes, and relax for a few minutes, enjoying a moment of peace. Even activities that require focus and attention can invigorate if they are pleasurable or interesting. A short walk in a nearby park may be just what you need—experiencing nature often has a natural revitalizing effect.

Exercise

Physical activity increases energy and contributes to well-being. When combined with a healthy diet and, if needed, weight loss, exercise lowers blood pressure and decreases the risk of heart disease. It's one of the keys to managing weight, reducing cholesterol, and controlling blood sugar. Exercise is also associated with improvement in mental function. Individuals who are active exhibit better mental processing speed and memory than their less active peers. Along with these health benefits, exercise has value in the workplace, as employees who are fit miss fewer days, are more satisfied with their jobs, and are more productive.

In 2011, the American College of Sports Medicine (ACSM) released exercise guidelines regarding the frequency, intensity, and duration of exercise in four areas: (1) cardiorespiratory, (2) resistance, (3) flexibility, and (4) neuromotor.

A *cardiorespiratory* exercise is any continuous and rhythmic activity involving large muscles that results in an increase in heart rate and respiratory rate—examples include swimming, brisk walking, jogging, and bicycling. The recommendation is 30 to 60 minutes of moderately intense exercise performed most days of the week, 20 to 60 minutes of vigorous exercise three or more days per week, or a combination of moderate and vigorous exercise three or more days per week. This guideline can be met in one setting or accumulated by engaging in multiple exercise sessions, each lasting 10 minutes or more. According to the ACSM, a moderately intense physical activity is one in which we work hard enough to increase our heart rate and break a sweat, but remain able to carry on a conversation.

In addition to cardiorespiratory exercise, the ACSM recommends strength training. By lifting weights or by exercising against *resistance*, we increase our strength and endurance. The current recommendation is two to four sets of 8 to 10 different exercises with 8 to 12 repetitions of each exercise on two or three nonconsecutive days each week. When building strength, the amount of weight or resistance used should result in substantial fatigue of the muscle group.

The ACSM also suggests that we do stretching exercises two to three days each week to promote the *flexibility* of all major muscle and tendon groups. Each exercise should be repeated two to four times (10 to 60 seconds per repetition). It's recommended that each stretching activity generate a feeling of tightness and mild discomfort. The target is 60 seconds of total stretching time for each muscle group. Stretching to promote flexibility is most effective when the muscle is first warmed through light-to-moderate cardiorespiratory activity or passively warmed via external methods such as moist heat or warm baths.

Neuromotor exercise focuses on the coordinated, simultaneous activity of multiple muscle groups. This type of activity improves balance, agility, muscle strength, coordination, and gait. The primary goal of neuromotor exercise is to improve overall daily physical function and the prevention of falls. Examples include yoga, tai chi, and Pilates. The current recommendation for these whole-body activities is two to three days each week for 20 to 30 minutes each day.

Reading these guidelines may leave you feeling a bit overwhelmed and discouraged. Who could meet all the recommendations? And even if you had the desire to achieve them all, who has the time? The good news is you don't have to meet all of them to benefit. Increasing your activity level, even if every requirement isn't met, will have a positive impact on your health. So walk one or two days a week, start cycling or jogging when you can, or hit the gym on the weekend. Keep the guidelines in mind, but don't beat yourself up for not meeting all of them. Increase your level of fitness guilt-free by making it more of a priority, adding the activities that work for you. It's worth it because even an incremental increase in exercise will benefit your health and enhance your energy level.

Nutrition

Eating well is a critical component of our health and productivity. Proper nutrition and avoiding excess pounds reduce the risk of hypertension, diabetes, heart disease, and sleep disturbances. Also, individuals who fail to manage this important energy source miss more time at work, spend more on health care, and are less able to meet the physical demands of their job.

To maintain a healthy diet, it's helpful to pay attention to three fundamental nutrients (macronutrients): carbohydrates, fats, and proteins.

Each of them is essential, but some dietary sources of these nutrients are better for us than others.

Carbohydrates are simple sugar molecules linked together in complex chains. When ingested, these chains are broken down into their component sugars, which are then absorbed into the bloodstream. Sugars are a valuable source of energy, powering a myriad of life-sustaining activities. In addition, the indigestible carbohydrates from plants are an important source of dietary fiber. Fiber is known to lower the risk of heart disease, diverticular disease (i.e., inflammation of the colon), and diabetes.

Of note, all dietary sources of carbohydrates are not the same—some are healthier for us than others. The key is the speed with which the sugars are broken down and absorbed. The carbohydrates with the most health benefits take the longest time to reach the bloodstream—the slower the better. The preferred dietary sources for these healthy, slowly-absorbed carbohydrates are fruits, vegetables, and whole grains, because these plant-based foods have the highest nutritional value and offer the added benefit of dietary fiber.

Interestingly, even when eating healthy sources of this nutrient, there is still a good bit of variability in how rapidly the carbohydrates are absorbed. The sugars in a piece of watermelon affect blood sugar differently than the ones found in an apple; the rise in blood sugar caused by raw carrots is different than that caused by boiled peas. Over the past several years, researchers have examined carbohydrate-rich foods with the goal of observing their impact on blood sugar. Each food that is tested is assigned a Glycemic Index (GI) number. The GI ranks foods on a scale from 0 to 100. The closer a particular food's GI is to 100, the more rapidly its carbohydrates are absorbed; the closer to 0, the more slowly they are absorbed. Based on this research, the GI for watermelon is 72, apples are 40, and raw carrots are 16. As indicated by these numbers, the carbohydrates from an apple are more slowly absorbed than those from watermelon, while raw carrots are very stingy when it comes to giving up their sugars. For a Web-based list of GIs for a particular food, see *www.glycemicindex.com*.

Some diets vilify *fats*, causing us to stand in line at the potato bar or bagel shop with the assumption that carbohydrates are better for us. But when it comes to dietary fat, abstinence isn't the answer. Rather, we benefit by choosing healthier fats. In particular, current recommendations suggest eating foods containing unsaturated fats (monounsaturated and polyunsaturated fats), while avoiding trans fats and limiting saturated fats.

Trans fats are generated when hydrogen is added to vegetable oils during a process called hydrogenation. Because they increase our risk for developing heart disease and diabetes, it's best to severely restrict their consumption. Prompted by these risks, the FDA requires manufacturers to provide trans fats information on the Nutritional Facts panel of all foods. Also, organizations like the Girl Scouts, McDonalds, and Wendy's have taken steps to reduce trans fats in the products they sell.

Similarly, it is important to limit saturated fats because, like trans fats, they are implicated in a wide variety of health problems. Saturated fats are found in meat (especially red meat), dairy products, and a few vegetable oils including palm and coconut oil.

In contrast to trans and saturated fats, the unsaturated fats found in plant oils, nuts, seeds, avocados, and fish have a more favorable health profile. Walter Willett, author of *Eat, Drink, and Be Healthy*, writes: "Cutting back on all types of fat and eating extra carbohydrates does little to protect against heart disease and will ultimately harm people. Instead, replacing saturated fats with unsaturated fats is a safe, proven, and delicious way to cut the rates of heart disease."

There are two dietary sources of *proteins*—animal and plant. The animal sources of protein include meat, fish, poultry, eggs, milk, and milk products. With animal proteins, however, it is easy to get too much saturated fat. To mitigate this problem, we can choose lean alternatives like fish, poultry, lean cuts of red meat, and low-fat milk and milk products and eat smaller portions. By eating low-fat protein sources, we can leverage the maximum health benefit while minimizing the risk associated with saturated fat.

Dietary proteins are also found in plants. Grains, legumes, nuts, and seeds are all excellent sources of this macronutrient. In addition, plants provide unsaturated fats, along with fiber, and a wide array of essential vitamins and minerals.

Proper nutrition is summarized by three easy-to-remember guidelines:

- Carbohydrates—Eat a variety of fruits, vegetables, and whole grains
- Fats—Eat unsaturated fats as the primary source of fat
- Proteins—Eat plant and low-fat animal sources of protein

Sleep

The demands of modern life make it difficult to get the rest we need. Work goals, family commitments, and personal interests all vie for our time, requiring us to squeeze as much as we can into each day. After our workday, there's homework to check, dinner to prepare, and yard work to complete, leaving limited time for enjoyable activities like reading or an evening stroll through the neighborhood. Even when intentionally restricting our sleep, we can't always cross off every item on our to-do list.

As a result of these many demands, rather than getting enough rest, we rely on coffee and energy drinks to keep us going. A large national survey found that 29.9 percent of U.S. workers and 40.5 percent of workplace managers aren't getting the recommended amount of sleep. Based on this data it is clear that America not only has a growing financial debt, it also has a growing sleep debt.

Individuals who fail to get enough sleep are putting themselves and others in danger. Failure to get adequate rest is associated with an increased risk of hypertension, heart disease, diabetes, and weight gain. In addition, insufficient sleep affects job performance and workplace safety. Fatigue and shift work are believed to have contributed to the nuclear power plant disasters at Three-Mile Island and Chernobyl, as well as the environmental destruction caused by the Exxon Valdez oil spill. Similarly, there is a peak in single motor-vehicle accidents at night. There is also an 18 percent increase in work-related incidents associated with human error on afternoon shifts and a 30 percent increase in such incidents on night shifts. Moreover, tired workers accomplish less. In one study, the annual cost due to fatigue-related productivity loss was estimated at $1,967 per employee. A healthy, safe, and productive workforce is fueled by sleep.

With this in mind, what's the optimal amount of sleep? While there's variability from one person to the next, the current recommendation from the National Sleep Foundation is seven to nine hours per night. In addition, a deficit accumulated over several nights can't be remedied with one night of extended sleep. It takes a consistent pattern of getting the required amount over a few days to fully recover.

Consider conducting your own experiment. Pay attention to the number of hours you sleep and monitor your level of fatigue. If you discover you are dragging most of the day, add some additional sleep time. Also, don't expect to feel equally energized at all times during the day. For many, based on the circadian rhythm, there's a natural dip in alertness that occurs in the early afternoon.

The Energized Leader

Over the next few days, perform your own personal energy audit:

- Overall are you energized, depleted, or somewhere in-between?
- How long can you work on a particular task before you began to lose focus?
- Which activities have the largest impact on your energy level?
- Are there certain times during the day when you feel more energized? (In general, are you a morning, afternoon, or evening person?)

Then, with your audit in mind, consider …

- Do you have enough *get tos* in your day? How many of your activities are *self-determined*—selected because you enjoy them for their own sake?
- Are your *connections* with others energizing?
- Does your day have enough time for rest and recovery? Do you unplug and take *breaks* from challenging tasks?
- Are you *exercising* enough?

- Are you eating well (proper *nutrition*)?
- Are you *sleeping* seven to nine hours each night?

As you reflect on these questions, consider what might need to change in order to add more energy to your life. If you are depleted and running on empty, adjust the structure of your day to include more activities that you find invigorating. Add more enjoyable pursuits—things you do for the simple satisfaction you gain from doing them. Spend time with others who energize you. Step back from projects when you begin to tire and your productivity declines. Exercise by taking a walk or jogging in the park. Be more intentional about eating well. Try to get enough sleep. Restructure your day and change your habits so you have a positive energy balance.

The Energized Team

Like individual energy, team energy is a renewable resource that varies from moment to moment with many peaks and valleys. At times, even enthusiastic, highly productive teams experience lows and, occasionally, periods of burnout. As a leader, one of your significant roles is to help energize the teams you lead. Whether you are leading a family, classroom, or work team, your ability to raise the excitement level will have a measurable impact on buy-in and success.

To create a positive energy balance, consider the following strategies: energy audit, job design, positive relatedness, and institutional support.

Energy Audit

A helpful starting point is an energy audit. Get to know what keeps the members of your team enthused about coming to work each day. Be as specific and concrete as possible; generalities aren't as useful as the particular activities that fill their tank. What excites them about a particular project? What is depleting? What kinds of tasks naturally capture their imagination?

It is also useful to get a sense for the ebb and flow of positive energy during the day. At what time of day do team members do their best work? How long can they focus on a task before they become distracted? How often do they need breaks?

An energy audit provides data that can be used to structure the workday and influence how jobs are assigned. If a team works best in the morning, schedule essential tasks early in the day, moving activities requiring less focus and energy to the afternoon. Teams that are at their best in two-hour blocks can plan breaks when focus begins to wane. Also, if there are projects that take a toll on morale and enthusiasm, the day can be arranged so that those tasks don't dominate—or they can be shared among multiple team members so that one individual isn't doing all the energy-depleting jobs.

Job Design

Jobs can be designed or redesigned in order to generate excitement. Tasks and projects with attributes like autonomy, competence, variety, meaning, challenge, and novelty naturally create a positive energy balance.

Autonomy: Self-determination is one of the most reliable antecedents of enthusiasm. In general, the more autonomy individuals experience the more productive they are. One of the most deflating behaviors a leader can engage in is micromanagement. When others feel they are being watched too closely or given too much instruction regarding how to accomplish a task, they lose motivation and disengage. Energy is created when leaders allow those they lead broad latitude in determining how to most effectively use their time.

Competence: Individuals are energized by activities they have mastered. The gifted communicator flourishes when she is in front of a group making a presentation. The detail person is at his best when he is developing and executing a complex, multifaceted strategic plan. Leaders contribute to a team's excitement by ensuring that, whenever possible, team members work in their areas of competence.

Variety: Team members function better when they have variety in their day. Too much of even a good thing can lead to a drop in performance. Following a break teams are often more focused, creative, and productive. A balance between engagement and stepping away for awhile often leads to better outcomes.

Meaning: Wasting time depletes energy. When individuals spend time working on tasks they don't value, or tasks unrelated to their success, they quickly lose interest and disengage. An important leadership role is to make sure team members are focusing their efforts on what really matters.

Challenge: As a general rule, we are attracted to activities that stretch us—calling out our very best. If we aren't appropriately challenged, we tend to experience boredom and begin to look for activities that will pique our interest.

Novelty: New experiences are naturally energizing. Recall the enthusiasm you experience beginning a new job or the first leg of a travel adventure. As a leader, whatever you can do to add newness to the day of those you lead will help them thrive, contributing to their productivity and satisfaction.

I'm aware there are no perfectly designed jobs—ones that are always exciting and never depleting. From time to time, even the most compelling projects and activities leave us feeling empty, and all we are able to do is put our head down and press forward with sheer will power. But to the extent we can help those we lead find autonomy, competence, variety, meaning, challenge, and novelty in their daily activities, they will be energized and perform at their best.

Positive Relatedness

As noted above, the way you relate to those you lead has a significant impact on their energy level. Relationships based on respect, empowerment, and trust create enthusiasm.

Respect: You can fuel the success of others by simply listening well. Whenever you meet with another person focus your mind, allow no interruptions or distractions, and listen carefully. Become totally absorbed in the conversation. Genuinely respect others by making each encounter your number-one priority.

Empowerment: Along with offering respect, do what you can to help others succeed. Frequently ask the question, "How can I help?"

Trust: Also, freely offer trust. Delegate tasks, share information, and encourage autonomy. The act of believing in another person boosts energy and instills a sense of confidence, leading to greater persistence and better performance.

Institutional Support

Individuals who feel supported are more energetic and productive. In a study of hotel service workers, the investigators observed that employees who felt their managers were supportive were more enthusiastic, dedicated, and engaged. These employees also provided better service and, interestingly, customers who interacted with them were more loyal to the hotel.

To add energy to the teams you lead, you might consider the question: "Am I doing what I can to help others succeed?" The assistance and support you provide can take many forms:

- It may consist of material resources, making sure others have what they require to function at the highest level.
- What is needed may be important information or specialized training.
- Sometimes the most supportive thing you can do is design tasks so they include autonomy, meaning, challenge, or novelty.

The goal is to take actions that demonstrate to team members you are firmly in their corner, ready to do whatever is necessary to help them reach their potential.

One Leader's Experience

A friend of mine works in labor relations as a contract negotiator. This is a high-stakes, pressure-cooker profession—parties are at odds, passions are high, and deadlines are tight. Yet to my amazement, he is uniquely able to maintain his own enthusiasm as well as the enthusiasm of his team. I asked him to share his secret—how is he able to energize the people he leads? He responded:

The best way I know to maintain the energy of my team is ...

- *Articulate a vision for them that will put their daily assignments in a larger context so that they understand there is real value in what they're doing*
- *Celebrate successes loudly, both individual successes and team successes*
- *Speak life into individual team members by calling out what is special about them and helping them understand how the team would suffer without their unique contributions*
- *Constantly be on the lookout for opportunities for each team member to do what he or she does best*

If all those things fail, I confess that I will bribe them with overpriced coffee, with excessive caffeine, whipped cream, and caramel. I'm not proud to admit that, but it works.

An Experiment

Below is a list of suggestions designed to energize both you and your team. Take a minute to look over this list and identify one or two of them you would like to try over the next two weeks.

Your Energy:

- *Self Determination*: In the next 24 hours, add one *get to*—something you do just because you love it.
- *Connections*: Spend time with someone who energizes you.
- *Breaks*: Add a new distraction to your day. Find a way to take a break that energizes you.
- *Exercise*: For the next two Saturdays, participate in an activity that meets one of the exercise recommendations identified in this chapter.
- *Nutrition*: For one meal each day, follow the nutrition guidelines suggested above.
- *Sleep*: For the next few days, make it a priority to sleep seven to nine hours each night.

Team Energy:

- *Energy Audit*: Ask the members of your team: "What current task or project is the most depleting and why?" "What current task or project is the most energizing and why?"
- *Job Redesign*: Ask the members of your team: "What job change, autonomy, competence, variety, meaning, challenge, or novelty would bring the most energy to the current project?"
- *Positive Relatedness*: Ask the members of your team: "Do you feel respected, empowered, and trusted?"
- *Institutional Support*: Ask the members of your team: "What can I do to help?" "What kind of support would be most beneficial?"

Approach this exercise as an experiment—alter your behavior and then observe what happens. Are you more energized? Are you more engaged and persistent? And what about those you lead? Are your teams more invested and productive?

KEY CONCEPTS

Energy is a valuable renewable resource

Without excitement and passion little of significance is ever accomplished. It's difficult to imagine success without an energized leadership and workforce. When we are focused and enthusiastic, we perform at our best.

Adding energy requires effort

It's often assumed that relaxation is the best way to fill our tank. It just seems right that a trip to the beach or spa is the best prescription for our energy needs. Yet, while undoubtedly important, that's only part of the equation. Frequently, the refreshment we need is found by engaging in interesting, meaningful, and challenging activities. We gain energy by expending it on what matters most.

COME
Undivided Attention
UP

FIVE

Undivided Attention

Our Greatest Gift

---

*"First of all," he said, "if you can learn a simple trick,
Scout, you'll get along a lot better with all kinds of folks.
You never really understand a person until you
consider things from his point of view ..."*
"Sir?"
"... until you climb into his skin and walk around in it."

—Harper Lee

In his book *Without Reservations*, J.W. (Bill) Marriott, Jr. offers his perspective on the backstory behind the phenomenal success of Marriott International. Beginning with his father, and then under his leadership, a business that started as a root beer stand grew into an industry-leading lodging company with, at the time of this writing, approximately 137,000 employees and more than 3,400 hotels in 68 countries and territories.

From Bill's perspective, Marriott's remarkable story is driven by a fundamental commitment to putting people first. Guided by this quintessential value, Bill's father, from the very beginning, built the family business around the pay-it-forward belief that if managers take care of their employees, their employees will take care of customers. Describing this approach in more detail, Bill makes the observation, "Nothing is as important as having managers in place who possess the people skills to support, encourage, lead, inspire, and listen to associates."

Further, he proposes, "Listening is the single most important on-the-job skill that a good manager can cultivate." Starting with senior leadership, Marriott's extraordinary growth is based on an organization-wide commitment to high-quality, caring relationships. The result of this relational focus is a positive work climate, invested employees, low turnover, and high employee satisfaction, which, in turn, drives customer service and, ultimately, brand loyalty.

Marriott's approach to leadership is effective because we, as humans, are inherently social. In all of us, there is an innate need to connect. Like a plant requires water, carbon dioxide, and nutrients from the soil, we require healthy relationships. Meaningful interactions with others are as important to our health and well-being as oxygen is to our survival.

The authors of a study published in *Science* concur, observing that "… social relationships, or the relative lack thereof, constitute a major risk factor for health—rivaling the effect of well-established health risk factors such as cigarette smoking, blood pressure, blood lipids, obesity, and [inadequate] physical activity." This observation is supported by another study based on a survey of 308,849 people. Its authors found that "… individuals with adequate social relationships have a 50% greater likelihood of survival compared to those with poor or insufficient social relationships. The magnitude of this effect is comparable with quitting smoking and it exceeds many well-known risk factors for mortality (e.g., obesity, physical inactivity)." There is clear and convincing evidence from these and countless other studies that positive interactions with others are foundational to health and well-being.

What is true for our personal health is equally true for the well-being and effectiveness of the teams we lead. The cohesiveness and functionality of families, sports teams, organizations, and even nations are dependent upon relationships. Highly successful endeavors are not built on the heroic actions of one person, but rather develop from the cooperative efforts of many working together, all aligned with a common vision and driven by a singular mission. When strife is the norm, failure inevitably follows. Incivility at work leads to absenteeism and decreased productivity. In contrast, engagement, productivity, and volunteerism increase when the members of a team enjoy one another's company. When relationships thrive, so do organizations.

Leadership is inherently relational. The primary means leaders have for influencing others is via their interactions. The most successful leaders relate well to others and build teams that work well together. A leader's LI—his or her capacity to bring out the best in others—is largely built upon the ability to initiate and maintain high-quality connections.

Connections Matter

I've had the good fortune to personally witness this dynamic. I very much enjoy serving on the trustee board of a Midwestern university, largely because of the individuals with whom I work. There is camaraderie in this group that is based on mutual respect and positive regard. Each person's perspective is valued, and everyone is encouraged to contribute. Care is commonly expressed by a genuine interest in each person's career and personal life.

The positive nature of the interactions not only adds to the pleasure of working together, but also contributes to our productivity. Relational trust and psychological safety provide the foundation for meaningful discussions, including difficult ones that might threaten the fabric of a less tight-knit group. The strong interpersonal bonds ensure civility regardless of the content of the conversation. As a result of the healthy connections that exist, the trustees serve the university more ably.

The efficacy of any group is profoundly influenced by the quality of the interactions among its members. Cohesive teams experience more positivity, attract better talent, and achieve more.

General intelligence refers to our capacity to perform mental tasks. It is an important aptitude that contributes to, among other things, our ability to excel at school and succeed in a wide variety of occupations. With respect to the teams we lead, there is a parallel capacity, called *collective intelligence*, which refers to a group's aptitude for executing activities like solving puzzles, brainstorming, making collective moral judgments, and negotiating over limited resources. It's an indicator of how well a group is able to work together in order to reach a common goal.

Collective intelligence is primarily built on two characteristics: social sensitivity and a willingness to take turns. When members of a group have an empathic understanding of one another, they form strong relational bonds and, as a result, achieve more. Further, groups that give every participant the opportunity to offer his or her perspective make a greater contribution than those in which one person dominates. Interestingly, a team's success is *not* strongly correlated with the general intelligence of individual members or the average general intelligence of the whole group. Thus, if, as leaders, we want a group to function at its best, it is not as important to get the smartest people in the room as it is to get the people in the room to work well with one another.

High-quality connections also contribute to our health and well-being. The workplace is frequently a demanding environment. There are deadlines to meet, superiors to keep happy, and multiple relationships to manage. When personal responsibilities are added to the mix, one can easily become overwhelmed. Our body's natural physiologic response to these everyday stresses is fight or flight. We automatically prepare to fend off an enemy or flee to safety. While gearing up to survive is perfectly suited for an adrenalin-laced encounter with our neighbor's overly aggressive dog, it's not so helpful when it occurs as the answer to the more typical long-term psychological stresses we experience in the modern workplace. Our innate physical response is adaptive when facing an acute, momentary crisis, but when a difficulty is prolonged it can harm our health and steal our joy.

Our response to stress, though automatic, is not immutable. It can be tempered by our relationships. While the pressures of life tend to increase heart rate and blood pressure, support from others has been shown to lower both of these indicators of the fight-or-flight response. Positive interactions also contribute to healthier levels of the stress hormone cortisol. Moreover, quality connections can enhance the immune system's ability to resist infection. In short, individuals with meaningful social ties are less physiologically responsive to the stress they encounter, resulting in better long-term health and well-being.

Unfortunately, all too often there is a more sinister side to our social interactions. Those we know best can cause as much or more stress than they alleviate. In stark contrast to positive interactions, incivility in a relationship is highly disruptive. Grit is exquisitely sensitive to negative exchanges. Disrespect and rudeness result in absenteeism, decreased productivity, and employee turnover. The authors of one study reported that individuals who were treated poorly at work lost work time worrying about the negative incident, wasted time trying to avoid the instigator, intentionally reduced their commitment to their organizations, and overall decreased their work effort. They simply stopped doing their best. When relationships break down, organizational dysfunction ensues. Little, if anything, causes disengagement and kills momentum like interpersonal strife.

Relationships matter. The quality of the connections within a group has a significant impact on well-being, positivity, and productivity.

Characteristics of Quality Connections

High-quality connections are based on characteristic ways of interacting. In this section, you will find five relational qualities that bring out the best in others: caring, understanding, appreciating, sharing, and trusting.

Caring

Healthy relationships are fundamentally dependent on a positive inclination toward others. Offering and receiving compassion and kindness is a basic human need. It's universal—everyone desires to have supportive people in their life. In a Gallup survey of 8 million workers, investigators found that employees who have a supervisor or co-workers who care about them are more productive and more likely to stay with an organization. Also, personnel who feel valued provide better customer service.

Care is based on an outward focus. It's built on a genuine interest in the well-being of others and an empathic understanding of their world. It's communicated by a desire to know what is going on in the life of another person and accompanied by a willingness to offer emotional and material support. We demonstrate our compassion by noticing when a coworker is overwhelmed or asking a mother or father, "How are your kids doing?"

One might think acts of kindness are intrinsically altruistic. That is, the one who offers care does it solely for the benefit of others while getting nothing in return. However, this is not the case. The gains are reciprocal—both giver and receiver get something from the interaction. The authors of a study investigating happiness asked study participants to keep track of every act of kindness they performed. At the end of the study period, those who had kept track were happier and more grateful than those who had not. Similarly, in his book *Flourish*, Martin Seligman writes: "… doing a kindness produces the single most reliable momentary increase in well-being of any exercise we have tested." Remarkably, even longevity is associated with caring. Individuals who offer support to friends and family live longer than their contemporaries who spend less time doing so.

Understanding

When we invest our time and energy getting to know others, a closeness results that forms the foundation for a cohesive and productive community. By carefully listening, we gain an appreciation for how the people around us view their current situation. In his book *The Road Less Traveled*, M. Scott Peck calls this process bracketing. He writes, "An essential part of true listening is the discipline of bracketing, the temporary giving up or setting aside of one's own prejudices, frames of reference and desires so as to experience as far as possible the speaker's world from the inside, stepping inside his or her shoes." This process of looking beyond our personal agendas and paying close attention promotes strong relational bonds.

In a study investigating social interactions and well-being, the investigators discovered that meaningful conversations and feeling understood and appreciated make the most consistent contribution to our sense of closeness with others. It seems, as a general rule, that people desire to be known. When an individual makes an effort to appreciate the viewpoint of another person, a relational bond is created—a bond that satisfies a fundamental need to feel connected.

One morning, at work, as I passed by a resident physician, I offered the socially scripted, obligatory, "How are you?" In response, she offered a lackluster, "Fine." On that particular day, I didn't accept her response at face value—it didn't seem authentic. What she was communicating verbally did not square with what she was communicating non-verbally. So, I stopped and tentatively suggested, "You don't seem fine."

This more empathic observation on my part resulted in a more heartfelt, verbal, and non-verbal response on her's. She paused, began to cry, and shared this was her first day back from maternity leave. Prior to coming to work, she had dropped off her child at day care for the very first time. She was experiencing guilt and a sense of loss for not being able to be with her child. At that point, the nature of our interaction had changed from scripted to meaningful. Because I had sensed a disconnect between her body language and her words and had taken the time to acknowledge her current situation, she shared more of her personal struggle. To be clear, I'm not the hero of this story; the hero is human understanding. A simple act of sensitivity to her plight created a connection.

One might argue that personal interchanges are a waste of time. After all, work is for work; not therapy. When on the company's dime, individuals ought to be doing their job, not sharing their feelings about the travails of parenting. And while I agree that the office or factory floor is not the place for psychotherapy, if a sense of human connection and community isn't established in the marketplace, satisfaction and performance predictably suffer. I am not talking about long interchanges processing personal issues, but rather brief moments characterized by empathy. Rather than being a distraction, exchanges focused on understanding create greater commitment to an organization and energize the workforce.

The positive impact of understanding is not limited to personal matters. Teams comprised of individuals who know each other well are better able to use everyone's strengths while minimizing weaknesses. Groups that value listening are able to leverage every person's input rather than being limited to the input of the most extroverted person. Time spent getting to know others adds to collective intelligence and leads to better decisions. Understanding brings out the very best in everyone involved. It's not a frivolous time waster; rather, it's a team-building exchange that contributes to organizational success.

Appreciating

As described in greater detail in the next chapter, productive teams have a six-to-one ratio of positive to negative interactions. Specifically, teams with social exchanges characterized by appreciation have more energy and are much more effective than teams with exchanges characterized by relational strain. Marcial Losada and Emily Heaphy, the authors who initially described this ratio, offer the following description of two very different work environments: "Qualitative observations of the teams showed that high-performance teams were characterized by an atmosphere of buoyancy that lasted during the whole meeting. By showing appreciation and encouragement to other members of the team, they created emotional spaces that were expansive and opened possibilities for action and creativity as shown in their strategic mission statements. In stark contrast, low-performance teams operated in very restrictive emotional spaces created by lack of mutual support and enthusiasm, often in an atmosphere charged with distrust and cynicism."

Similarly, based on their survey of more than 15 million employees worldwide, Gallup researchers suggest that the number-one reason people leave their job is they don't feel appreciated. Recognition contributes significantly to the positive feelings experienced within any organization. Workers who believe their contributions are valued are more productive and engaged. They also have better safety records, and the customers they interact with are more loyal and satisfied.

Diana, a market manager for one of America's largest financial institutions, has experienced, firsthand, the critical importance of caring for and appreciating employees at all strata of an organization. In an e-mail correspondence, she wrote:

Most industry experts would agree that banking is all about relationships, including relationships between managers and their subordinates. But with the long checklist of procedures, processes, security, audits, and most importantly, profitability and sales, many times, the importance of relationships with employees falls to the bottom of the priority list. When one has responsibility for 100 branches in a highly competitive market, finding time to develop high-quality connections with each employee can be a challenge. When I was promoted into the position of market manager, most of my colleagues were traditional bankers who had "grown up" in banking and finance. Quality interactions weren't necessarily their strong suit. My background was relationship sales where the focus was on people and their needs.

As a market manager, one of my responsibilities was visiting branches to ensure that each one was performing at its best. It was typical for my counterparts to make a beeline to the branch president's office without meeting or even acknowledging other job families like tellers, customer service representatives, and bankers. My approach was different. I nurtured strong relational bonds with all job families to model caring and appreciation for each individual and his or her contribution to the team. It required doing homework and collecting information about their personal lives and recent achievements prior to the branch visit, to increase the possibility of connecting on a personal level. I wanted to communicate my care for them before focusing on the business at hand. This relational approach paid great dividends—within a year, my market was ranked number one nationally.

High-quality interactions not only make sense from a relational and employee satisfaction perspective, but also from a bottom-line perspective. Connecting with employees on a personal level generates success on every level. It is just good business!

Sharing

Cohesive groups celebrate success by retelling it. The impact of a positive experience is augmented and extended when it's shared. The process of repeating what has occurred causes a reliving of the moment along with its associated feelings.

However, sharing is only the beginning. How others respond determines what happens next. If they passively ignore what is shared, the positive impact of an accomplishment is diminished. Similarly, destructive responses completely spoil the moment—negativity trumps positivity every time. In contrast, when others respond enthusiastically with focused interest, the good mood is extended. By listening carefully, asking questions, and taking interest in what is revealed, the conversation continues and the feelings are re-experienced.

For example, if a coworker shares with you how pleased she is with a recent presentation at work, and you respond by changing the topic, your words will diminish her excitement and joy. Or, if you find fault, pointing out even just one deficiency, it will immediately hijack the mood. But if you listen carefully, you will extend her positivity and sense of accomplishment. By actively engaging and celebrating, you are strengthening your connection and, in the process, making her day.

Good news needs to be shared and celebrated. Do what you can to capitalize and extend the positivity that occurs in your life by talking about it. When others reveal their successes, congratulate them. Take a genuine interest in their triumphs. Don't let any fortuitous happening pass by without showing enthusiasm, finding out more, and offering kudos. Celebration leverages every last bit of positivity from the good things that occur and builds energized and highly productive individuals and teams.

Trusting

Erik Erikson, a well-known developmental psychologist, proposes that between birth and 18 months a child develops either a basic trust in others and the environment or, unfortunately, a basic mistrust. Every newborn is completely dependent upon caregivers for his or her survival. As a result, an infant's perceptions of the safety and predictability of the world are determined by the quality of care that he or she receives. Children who are fed when hungry and comforted when frightened learn to trust that the world is a safe place. As a consequence, they freely explore and readily form meaningful attachments with others. An offspring who trusts willingly jumps from the edge of the swimming pool into his dad's outstretched arms, taking the risk because he is confident his parent will protect him from harm. However, when fundamental needs are not consistently met, mistrust develops and the environment is deemed unpredictable and dangerous. Others are viewed as unreliable, and rewards and punishments are perceived as capricious. A child who mistrusts has difficulty forming attachments and is more cautious.

One's capacity to trust continues to have a major influence on feelings, thoughts, and actions at every stage of life. In adulthood, it provides the psychological and social safety net necessary to form meaningful relationships.

Trust is both a character trait (trustworthy) and a way of interacting (trusting):

- People build trust by acting in a trustworthy manner. They are dependable, consistently doing what they say they will do. Regardless of the external circumstance, their behavior is predictably guided by clear values. They are benevolent, wanting others to succeed. In addition, those who are trustworthy don't undermine the efforts of others. They don't respond to missteps and mistakes in a punitive manner; nor do they publicly embarrass or criticize.
- In addition to being a character trait, trust is a way of acting toward others. It's readily delegating important projects and tasks. It means allowing those you lead to choose how they will approach a given activity without micromanaging. Trust is also established by providing resources. Others feel that you believe in them when they are given the assets they need. Further, trust is demonstrated by listening in a non-defensive manner. A trusting individual is teachable—open to feedback and ready to act on input from others.

Trust creates a safe and productive environment. Team members who are comfortable with each other are willing to work together in the pursuit of common goals.

Caring, understanding, appreciating, sharing, and trusting all contribute to the formation of high-quality connections. Interactions based on these characteristics help each of us reach our potential.

Relational Leaders

Leaders have a significant influence on the nature of the relationships that develop within the teams they lead. In this section, we will explore four pathways designed to initiate and sustain strong relational bonds: undivided attention, positive perceptions, consistent encouragement, and meaningful challenge.

Undivided Attention

I have come to believe that listening is the single most effective way to bring out the best in family, friends, and colleagues. When we pause, set ourselves aside, and make the effort to empathize with the people in our lives, we communicate a willingness to connect and make a meaningful investment. By offering our undivided attention, we clearly convey our respect and send the message that the thoughts and feelings of others matter.

The primary reason we listen is to gain an appreciation for the perspective of those with whom we interact. Perspective taking is the "capacity to consider the world from another individual's viewpoint." It's the ability to know how events are affecting others, making the connection between occurrences and the impact of those occurrences.

Taking the time and putting forth the effort to get to know others strengthens our relationships. When we comprehend, even imperfectly, the thoughts and feelings of those with whom we share life, we are better able to interact in a manner that is congruent with their current state. Knowing another's world builds empathy, positivity, and contributes to the clarity of communication. The more we appreciate how others view the world and their current situation, the easier it is to know when to celebrate, when to challenge, and when to simply listen. Although it's impossible to completely understand another person's perspective, merely making the effort to "walk around in his or her shoes" will be seen as an emotional investment that is certain to pay dividends.

While I believe in the value of undivided attention, I must confess that I don't always act in a manner congruent with my belief. There is frequently a disconnect between what I believe and how I act. At times, I'm distracted and don't focus on the person in front of me. Sometimes I have an agenda, or I'm impatient, wanting to guide the conversation to a desired end. Other times I'm simply tired. Yet, when I do make the time to pause and listen, the impact on my connections with others is noticeable, if not dramatic. I am healthier and so are those with whom I'm talking. And if we are engaged in a project at work, everyone is more productive.

Let me suggest, if you aren't already doing so, that you make a conscious effort to offer undivided attention, especially to those individuals who look to you for leadership. Over the next few days, make it your priority to understand how others view themselves and their situation. Listen with the intent of seeing the world as they see it. Allow what you learn to inform your words and actions. Celebrate with those who are celebrating. Offer words of encouragement to peers who are having a lousy day. Then, observe the impact on your relationships. Does it add value to the time you spend with others? Does it bring out the best in your colleagues?

Positive Perceptions

As with undivided attention, positive perceptions build strong relational bonds. In a study of couples who had been together for, on average, 10.9 years, the investigators observed that a benevolent bias predicted relational satisfaction.

As part of their participation in this research project, couples were asked to rate themselves and their partners on a number of virtues like kindness, openness, warmth, and sociability. Also, a friend of each couple was asked to rate each of the partners on an identical list of virtues. What the investigators found is fascinating. They discovered that individuals who rated their partner higher than the partner rated him or herself were happier in their marriages. And, similarly, individuals who rated their partner higher than the partner was rated by a friend had stronger, more satisfying relationships. In short, the couples who perceived the best in each other had stronger marital bonds. The authors concluded: "The results revealed that intimates in satisfying marriages perceive more virtue in their partners than their friends or their partners themselves perceive. They also possess partners who see them in this benevolently distorted light."

One might assume that realistic perceptions would result in better interactions with others. Conventional wisdom suggests that seeing things as they "really" are is always superior. However, this doesn't appear to be the case. In relationships, research suggests that idealism is associated with more beneficial outcomes than realism. The strongest, most satisfying social connections are predicated on positive biases. Self-fulfilling prophecy appears to be at work. If one expects good things from others, they will respond by being their best. Also, a benevolent bias leads to greater commitment and resiliency. In relationships in which the best is assumed, the failings or perceived failings of others are better tolerated. When family members or colleagues disappoint, as they inevitably do, these disappointments are interpreted as being the result of transient situational variables—not stable character flaws. By offering the benefit of the doubt, normal strains in a relationship are tempered, minimizing the impact of setbacks. In addition, anticipating the best builds self-esteem. Individuals are prone to feel better about themselves when others view them in a good light. Positive perceptions of others lead to stronger bonds, less conflict, and greater satisfaction.

Consider your own experience. How do you view the individuals in your network? Is there a particular person you view as irritable, argumentative, and rude? If so, do these perceptions influence your willingness to collaborate? Do you ever find yourself avoiding this person? Conversely, if you view one of your colleagues as intelligent, ethical, and compassionate, what impact do these perceptions have on your interactions with him or her? Are you more willing to invest?

To be clear, I'm not saying healthy perceptions are devoid of reality. Nor do I believe one benefits by being naïve and assuming the best despite consistent evidence to the contrary. Rather, I'm suggesting there is value in beginning with assumptions that are benevolently distorted. By believing the best, one creates expectancies that strengthen relationships and call forth the very best from others.

Consistent Encouragement

Leaders encourage others by what they say and do. Words are powerful—with them one can enhance self-esteem and motivate high-level achievement or one can discourage and demotivate. Depending on what is said, an individual can build a tight-knit group or create relational rifts. Phrases like, "You're making a valuable contribution," "Your effort is appreciated," and "I'm grateful for your help" contribute to positivity and cohesiveness. People are more connected and are more willing to invest when those with whom they interact offer verbal encouragement.

Leaders also encourage others by what they do. In practical terms, one of the most effective ways a leader can inspire a team is to enable progress. When managers remove barriers and provide resources, they concretely demonstrate their support and willingness to help. Along with material support, leaders enable progress by providing information, instruction, and feedback. Knowledge is often a critical factor that determines which initiatives succeed. When employees are provided with relevant data, they feel a stronger linkage with their superiors and are more willing to invest. Helping others succeed is a source of encouragement and, as a result, builds strong relational bonds and highly effective teams.

Meaningful Challenge

Being attentive, positive, and encouraging in relationships doesn't preclude challenging others to do and be their best. High-quality connections aren't solely predicated on mega doses of unexamined positivity—all smiles, hugs, and pats on the back. In fact, meaningful challenge is a necessary component of any long-term affiliation. As noted in Chapter One, developing one's competencies meets a very fundamental human need. Healthy, growing individuals possess an inner desire to be productive and achieve excellence. Leaders who challenge others to meet high standards of character and performance are helping those they lead experience satisfaction and reach their potential.

A popular view of goal setting suggests that moderately difficult challenges are the most motivating. According to this theory, when the probability of success is moderate—not too high or too low—individuals will exert the most effort. Goals that are too difficult are thought to demotivate; while goals with a high probability of success aren't challenging enough. However, research in the behavioral sciences does not support this theory. Rather it supports the view that difficult challenges are the most motivating. Assuming an individual has the necessary skills and a desire to get better, difficult tasks generate the greatest effort and lead to the highest level of achievement.

With this in mind, as a leader, set the bar high for yourself and others. Stand out in what you do. Ask your sales associates to go for it. Expect your analysts to excel. This is not to say one ought to be a merciless taskmaster, constantly pushing and haranguing. Challenge is not the same as browbeating; nor should it be accompanied by incivility. Rather, it's best received in the context of positive, high-quality connections. Asking others to get on board and work hard is most effective when it's seamlessly integrated with undivided attention, positive perceptions, and consistent encouragement. Set high standards, but be sure to set them in a positive relational context. Be the kind of person others want to join in the mutual pursuit of meaningful ends.

Undivided attention, positive perceptions, consistent encouragement, and meaningful challenge are all pathways that lead to high-quality connections. When these pathways are well travelled, the result is a safe interpersonal space that fosters grit and productivity.

Relational Teams

With these pathways to strong relational bonds in mind, let me suggest the following ways a leader can facilitate healthy interactions: model it, teach it, expect it, and acknowledge it.

Model it: As a leader, set the example. Be the first to offer undivided attention, support, and trust. By modeling positive interactions, an environment is created that encourages others to develop their own healthy connections.

Teach it: Along with modeling positive interactions, it's also helpful to provide instruction and feedback. An individual's capacity to relate well to others, like most any skill, benefits from instructional input. The information offered need not take place in a formal lecture or a seminar. In fact, the most effective teaching frequently occurs in the context of individual coaching or mentoring. As you walk to lunch, debrief after a meeting, or make your way to the parking lot, share ideas regarding ways to build strong relational bonds.

Expect it: Don't settle for less than high-quality interactions. Expect those you lead to trust, care, understand, and celebrate with one another. When there is incivility, address it privately, immediately, and directly. Don't allow negative interactions to occur without taking corrective action.

Acknowledge it: As a leader, when you observe a positive interaction, don't let it pass unnoticed. Affirm others for their efforts to encourage those they work with. When team members offer support or demonstrate care, be sure to recognize their actions. When individuals take the perspective of their peers or volunteer to help, let them know how beneficial their actions are in building team chemistry. Create the expectation that positive interactions will be acknowledged.

By promoting high-quality connections, leaders bring out the best in others. Strong relational bonds are created when healthy interactions are modeled, taught, expected, and acknowledged. The end result is a cohesive team whose members work well together, achieve more, and enjoy being with each other. Teams thrive when relationships thrive.

One Leader's Experience

A high-capacity leader I know is a self-described multitasker known for carrying on conversations while simultaneously responding to text messages and answering e-mails. What follows is a description of what occurred when she decided to change her relational and leadership style:

Let's just say that God developed me with an overactive mind and heart. I move, live and breathe a bit faster than your average person—not better, just faster. This can make for productive workdays and a strong ability to manage and multitask, but at times I can also forget to pause and be present when interacting with others. In an effort to be more present, I decided to work on putting down what I'm working on, turn my body away from my computer (phone or tablet), make eye contact with anyone who wandered into my office and actively listen. I decided to try to offer my undivided attention—for a full week.

Wow! This radically changed my work experience! I actually felt more productive because I was able to connect with those I work with on a deeper level. There was more grace and flexibility on all fronts. As I began to really listen, the employees who report to me actually needed my attention less because they were getting all of their questions answered in one dose. Our team meetings were more uplifting and energizing. And later in the week I was even able to follow up with a few of them to ask about the personal and family concerns they had mentioned earlier in the week.

Such a simple change. What a big impact.

An Experiment

In this chapter, I propose that a leader's capacity to bring out the best in others is fundamentally linked to his or her ability to relate well. By freely offering undivided attention, positive perceptions, consistent encouragement, and meaningful challenge, leaders create strong interpersonal bonds characterized by caring, understanding, appreciating, sharing, and trusting. When positive interactions are the norm, a climate is created that allows individuals to reach their full potential.

Below is an exercise designed to facilitate the development of high-quality connections. Let me suggest that you conduct your own experiment. Give the activities described in this exercise a try and, after a few days, observe the impact on your relationships. Is there more positivity? Do team members enjoy being together? Is there a spirit of volunteerism?

The Relational Leader:

- At the end of your day, review your interactions, focusing on the ones that strengthened your connections with others. Identify the specific exchanges that contributed to the caring, understanding, appreciating, sharing, and trusting you experienced. As you assess a particular encounter, consider the following questions:
  - What was it about the interaction that strengthened your relationship?
  - Was it strengthened by undivided attention, positive perceptions, consistent encouragement, meaningful challenge, or something else?
- Then, each day, identify one new way to support and encourage others.

The Relational Team:

- At the end of your day, review the interactions that occurred between members of the teams you lead. Identify the specific exchanges that contributed to the caring, understanding, appreciating, sharing, and trusting you observed. As you assess a particular exchange, consider the following questions:
  - What was it about the interaction that strengthened the relational bond?
  - Was it strengthened by undivided attention, positive perceptions, consistent encouragement, meaningful challenge, or something else?
- Then, challenge team members to find at least one new way to support and encourage their peers.

KEY CONCEPTS

Leadership is inherently relational

Our capacity to lead well is largely determined by our interactions with others. If those we lead feel cared for and supported, they will invest more and find greater satisfaction in their efforts.

Work relationships are important determinants of grit and success

High-quality connections bring out the best in all of us. Success is a byproduct of team cohesiveness. When we enjoy the people we work with, we are more persistent and, as a result, achieve more. Conversely, relational strife leads to disengagement, turnover, and lost productivity.

Undivided attention is a fundamental relationship-building skill

All of the interpersonal skills identified in this chapter are based on listening, a quality that is essential to any healthy relationship. Undivided attention is the price of admission. It's the initial step in every meaningful interaction.

COME

UPositivity

SIX

Positivity

The Power of Positive Feelings

Happy employees produce more than unhappy ones over the long term. They routinely show up at work, they're less likely to quit, they go above and beyond the call of duty, and they attract people who are just as committed to the job. Moreover, they're not sprinters; they're more like marathon runners, in it for the long haul.

—Gretchen Spreitzer & Christine Porath

As I was writing this chapter, one of my friends was showing a video of his six-week-old child's first smile to anyone (and everyone) who would watch. In this video, his wife was cooing and smiling, and their son was reciprocating with his own adorable toothless grin. As I observed this proud parental display, I was struck by the universal impact—invariably, every person who watched reflexively smiled. Regardless of gender, age, socioeconomic status, or race—and no matter what was going on at that moment in time—each individual stopped what he or she was doing and responded in kind. Two weeks later, I saw this young family out in public. As before, everyone who came near this exuberant child mirrored his expression.

Emotions of all kinds spread from one person to the next—they're contagious. In a study conducted in Sweden, investigators examined what occurs when we encounter another person who is expressing either a positive or a negative feeling. The participants in this experiment viewed pictures of happy and angry faces. When they looked at a happy face, they instinctively smiled; when exposed to an angry face, they instantly frowned. Remarkably, their responses, smiling or frowning, occurred even before they were consciously aware of what they had seen. The transfer of emotion was automatic and immediate.

This unconscious transmission of feelings was also observed many years ago in a small town in Massachusetts. In 1948, the National Heart Institute initiated an ambitious research project known as the Framingham Heart Study, the primary purpose of which was to identify the risk factors associated with heart disease. A lesser known, but equally significant, purpose was to examine happiness from a social perspective. Based on data from 4,739 individuals, researchers made the observation that the closer we are geographically to another individual, the more likely we will be influenced by his or her mood. This study suggests that if we desire happiness, we should surround ourselves with happy people.

Emotions are not only contagious in communities like the one studied in the Framingham Heart Study, but also in our homes and in organizations of all kinds. To test this hypothesis for yourself, think back to the last time you were in a meeting with someone in a truly bad mood; perhaps they were irritable or overly critical. How long did it take for the black cloud of negativity to sour your outlook—or even enlarge to the point that it darkened the entire room? Conversely, recall a meeting in which one of the participants was genuinely positive; not boisterous or obnoxiously energetic, but appropriately upbeat? Did that person's demeanor have any impact on what occurred?

For better or worse, as leaders, we set the tone. An organization's emotional climate is influenced from the top.

The Positivity Advantage

One might wonder if it really matters. Is positivity worth transmitting? Just because emotions like amusement, awe, and inspiration are communicable, are they necessarily beneficial? Certainly, there are many things we catch from others that we wish we wouldn't—like the flu, for example.

With respect to positivity, however, the data is clear: It does indeed make a beneficial difference. It offers a distinct advantage mentally, emotionally, socially, and physically. In fact, research consistently demonstrates that positive individuals …

- perform better in their jobs
- receive more favorable evaluations
- support their co-workers
- are persistent when attempting difficult tasks
- experience greater satisfaction at work
- make more money

At the beginning of her career, one highly effective secondary school teacher I know was advised to spend as much time as possible with peers who were upbeat and constructive. During an orientation session for her first job, a senior colleague told her group of assembled rookies that the best advice one could offer regarding how to become a great teacher had nothing to do with pedagogy. Rather, that if these new teachers wanted to excel at the highest level, they should deliberately surround themselves with positive people instead of negativistic or burned out co-workers. This veteran teacher understood, on a very practical level, the infectious nature of emotions and their link to excellence in the classroom.

In addition to contributing to work-related success, positive feelings have a significant impact on individual health and well-being. Happy individuals …

- have more meaningful and satisfying relationships
- experience fewer physical complaints
- cope better with illness
- report less depression

Positivity even offers protection from the common cold.

Sheldon Cohen, from Carnegie Mellon University, measured the level of positive emotions in 193 volunteer adults between the ages of 21 and 55. He then deliberately infected them with a cold virus and quarantined them for the next five days. What he then observed is fascinating. Positive participants developed fewer observable signs and symptoms of illness. They had less nasal congestion, sneezing, runny nose, sinus pain, and sore throat. It was as if positivity had immunized them against this annoying illness.

And if our basic health can be influenced by our emotional state, what about longevity? In a study of Major League Baseball players, Ernest Abel and Michael Kruger identified a link between a player's smile and the length of his life, finding that players who had a full smile in a photograph taken when they were young men lived an average of seven years longer than the players who didn't smile.

This same dynamic was observed in a group of women. In particular, young women who were more positive, as indicated by their smiles captured in college yearbook pictures, experienced fewer psychological and social difficulties as adults, had better relationships with others, and generally felt more satisfied with their lives than women who were not smiling in their photos. As they grew older, these happy coeds were also more likely to be satisfied in their marriages.

A positive outlook also benefited a group of nuns from the Midwest. In 1930, at an average age of 22, these religious devotees were asked to write brief autobiographical statements. More than 60 years later, Deborah Danner and her colleagues examined what had been written with the goal of determining if there was a connection between the age of a nun when she died and the emotional content of her autographical statement written many years earlier. Remarkably, the researchers found that individuals who had written statements high in positive content lived up to ten years longer than those who had expressed the least positivity.

There is clear and consistent evidence that positive emotions contribute to our well-being and fuel our success. They add richness and satisfaction to our personal lives, enhance our meaningful connections with others, and boost our performance at work.

More About Emotions

Research in the social sciences suggests that positive and negative emotions are *not* simply different ends of the same continuum. Happiness is not a lack of sadness, serenity is not the opposite of anxiety, and love is certainly more than a lack of hatred.

What we are learning is that negative emotions warn us about specific threats, focus our attention, and narrow our response repertoire. When we experience bad feelings, our bodies automatically and immediately mobilize resources to support quick, survival-promoting actions. When angry, we are instantly ready to attack. When anxious, we will go to great lengths to avoid whatever is causing our discomfort—spiders, mice, and snakes come to mind. When surprised or frightened, we react with fight or flight. Negative emotions are limiting. They make our world smaller, which is beneficial—life-saving, even—when under immediate threat of attack, but not so much so in the relatively safe environment of our day-to-day experience.

Whereas negativity narrows our perspective, positivity elicits a very different response, motivating us to *broaden* our understanding and *build* on our experience. It opens our intellect to new possibilities, leading to better problem solving and enhanced creativity. We naturally turn toward that which is positive, opening our minds to take in as much as we are able. It inspires us to actively seek opportunities and to interact more richly with our environment. Positive emotions help us adapt to and recover more quickly from negative experiences. They make a significant contribution to our intellectual, physical, social, and psychological resources.

I have experienced the broadening and building impact of positive emotions in both my personal and professional life.

- The awe I experience hiking in the mountains compels me to go back and seek the next adventure.
- The satisfaction I feel when completing a difficult task at work motivates me to work harder, learn more, and develop additional skills in order to meet the next challenge.

- Gratitude for what others do for me draws me closer to those I care about, building social interactions that promote health and well-being.

My life is richer and I have more resources because of the awe, satisfaction, and gratitude I experience. These benevolent feelings add to my vitality and bring out the best in me.

Positivity opens us up to a myriad of possibilities. It enhances our interactions with others and makes us more aware of the richness of our surroundings—creating an upward spiral, which promotes health and well-being, as well as greater productivity and success.

It Should Be Easy

If positivity is all that is required for us to lead others well and reach our potential, it should be easy, right? Common sense tells us joy, serenity, and hope ought to be life's default path, requiring little, if any, effort. In this case, however, our common sense results in the wrong conclusion. The fact is that positivity is elusive. It's hard to come by because bad is stronger than good, adaptation is the norm, energy is required, and prediction is imperfect.

Bad Is Stronger Than Good

When compared with positive events, negative events have a more pronounced and lasting impact. The soldier exposed to a horrific battle lasting only a few minutes can be affected for the remainder of his life. The child victimized by abuse can face significant issues well into adulthood. There is little, if any, doubt that traumatic experiences are life altering. In contrast, while the effects of trauma are enduring, there is no comparable counterpart when it comes to positive experiences. No matter how much pleasure we gain from a particular occurrence in our lives, the emotions we feel are fleeting—lasting for a brief moment and then they are gone.

Even when we look at more mundane day-to-day happenings, the impact of negative incidents lasts longer and is felt more intensely. A thoughtless, angry word from a friend can literally end that friendship, while the effect of a kind word is temporary, passing quickly as we move on. A botched presentation at work may become the focus of our obsession for days, while the afterglow of a successful project often fades as soon as we begin to focus on the next item on our agenda. The beautiful, awe-inspiring sunrise we see during our morning commute is gone the instant we are cut off in traffic. We are wired to feel more intensely and think more critically about our negative experiences.

Adaptation Is the Norm

Remaining positive is also difficult because we rapidly adapt to the good things that happen. A pay raise feels great for a bit, but its luster soon fades because our standard for what is required to make us happy also increases. Our first kiss is unforgettable, but what about the second, the third, or the $10,000^{th}$?

Even individuals who have won the lottery adjust quickly to their newfound wealth. While they experience momentary joy and elation, those feelings simply do not last. When compared with non-winners, instant millionaires report less pleasure in ordinary activities of daily life such as talking with a friend, watching television, eating breakfast, receiving a compliment, or buying new clothes. So, despite their financial windfall, lottery winners are no more positive and, in fact, they experience less pleasure than peers who have not shared their good fortune.

Energy Is Required

It takes attention and effort to remain positive. Daily irritations can easily derail our most earnest desire to have a good day. We may wake up in the morning with every intention of remaining upbeat; but, as our day progresses, our energy wanes and our joy gets hijacked. The stress of work and the demands of family take their toll, enabling negativity to creep in. As we grow weary from dealing with the difficulties of our day, we become impatient with others. The serenity we once felt is a distant memory.

Prediction Is Imperfect

Moreover, we are not very accurate prognosticators of what will make us happy. We assume that more money, a new home, or a girlfriend will be just what we need to experience the peace and contentment we desire. Or maybe we think losing a few pounds or a move to a new part of the country will elevate our mood. Unfortunately, it doesn't work this way. We are not good forecasters of how we will be affected by a particular event. Like wanderers in a desert who discover the oasis in the distance is only a mirage, we can spend an inordinate amount of time pursuing goals that, when achieved, do not have the desired impact.

How about you? Are you good at knowing what will make you happy? Have you ever wanted something badly, worked hard to reach a goal, or invested a great deal of material resources, only to obtain what you wanted and find it didn't elicit the pleasure or elevate your mood as much as you thought it would?

It's not easy to remain positive—peace, awe, and satisfaction are fleeting. If we are not vigilant and intentional, the bad we experience can overwhelm the good.

3 to 1 … 5 to 1 … 6 to 1

So what's the solution—how do we remain emotionally upbeat when that is not necessarily our natural bent? I believe the answer lies, at least partially, in intentionally cultivating feelings like interest, hope, and love. That is, we can best overcome negativity with frequent doses of positivity.

3 to 1: In her research on emotions, Barbara Fredrickson, the Kenan Distinguished Professor at the University of North Carolina, has identified a ratio that predicts positivity. She has observed that individuals with a positive bent typically experience at least three positive occurrences for every negative one. These individuals have mastered the art of cherishing all that is good, seeking meaningful interactions, and mindfully savoring positive happenings. The result is a rich, more personally fulfilling life and growing connections with others.

5 to 1: A similar ratio has been identified in healthy relationships. John Gottman, in his book *What Predicts Divorce*, notes that relationships predominated by nurturing interactions are more satisfying and last longer. According to Gottman, the ratio of positive to negative found in stable relationships is five to one. That is, those spouses who relate well to one another offer five positive interactions for every negative one.

6 to 1: Positivity is also a hallmark of high-performance teams. A study of 60 management teams from a large information-processing corporation found that teams with more positive interactions significantly outperformed their less cheery counterparts. Teams with members who expressed support or appreciation six times more frequently than they expressed disapproval, sarcasm, or cynicism generated more profit, had higher customer satisfaction ratings, and better job evaluations. This six-to-one ratio resulted in a better work environment and better performance.

After hearing about all the benefits of positivity, one might wonder: Is it possible to be too positive? Although this question has not been rigorously studied, the answer is likely, yes. If we are too Pollyanna-like or annoyingly happy, we may be disregarded by others as inane or unrealistic. If we do not listen to corrective feedback, we may blissfully ignore important deleterious realities and, as a result, make mistakes harmful to ourselves and the entities we lead.

To be clear, I'm *not* suggesting we paste a silly grin on our face and naively ignore negative feedback. Being positive is not a call to smile as we bury our heads in the sand and run our lives into the ground; rather it's a call to approach all of life, the good and the bad, with a positive bent. The goal is not to ignore problems but to employ a benevolently biased outlook as we address challenges with steeled determination. Positivity is a resource that helps us actively and creatively overcome barriers, making us more resilient as we face the problems that inevitably come our way.

The Positive Leader

As we have seen, positivity is a valuable asset. It inspires buy-in and drives productivity. In this section, we will explore ways to become more upbeat as a leader. Specifically, what I am discovering is we can become more positive by making a habit of savoring, seeking, and sharing.

Savoring

If you're not currently doing so, deliberately slow your pace and focus your mind on the good in your day. Nothing is too small to notice. It may be a kind word from a friend. You might receive pleasure from a customer's smile or, perhaps, something as seemingly mundane as the coffee that greets you each morning when you arrive at work.

In a complex, fast-paced world, it's easy to go through our day without really paying attention. Busyness distracts us, and we miss out on the small pleasures that are all around. For many of us, positive, life-enhancing experiences are so much a part of the fabric of our typical day that they fade unnoticed into the background. We miss the exuberance of our children because we are trying to get them ready for school and get ourselves to work. We respond to our colleague's success with a disinterested "that's nice," because of the time press created by our to do list.

Try to resist this sinister tendency; learn to pause and be mindful of positive experiences—the large and the small. Stay in the moment, fully engaged in whatever is in front of you at any given point in time. Eat mindfully, appreciating every smell, taste, and texture. Engage in meetings, regardless of how mundane the agenda might be. Make every conversation count.

In addition to savoring experiences as they happen, you can extend the positivity you feel by reliving them. At the end of your day, mentally review what occurred in your life; selectively focusing on the events and activities that elicited feelings of gratitude, amusement, or awe. Take the time to recall all the details and emotions of these positive experiences. What time was it? What were you doing? Where were you? Who were you with? And, importantly, how were you feeling? Don't overanalyze or critique what happened, just rewind the experience and relive the moment.

Seeking

Each of us has our own unique set of likes—activities we are drawn to. How about you? What are yours?

- What inspires you the most? Is it a good book, a mentor's encouragement, or a friend's remarkable accomplishment?
- Currently, what activities in your life are especially satisfying? Jogging in the park? Leading a productive meeting?
- What are you most grateful for? Maybe friends, family, or your job come to mind.

As you consider these questions, generate a list of experiences that contribute to your positivity. Based on what you know about yourself, what elicits feelings like joy, hope, or serenity within you? To jumpstart your thinking, take a quick look at some activities others have found useful in their pursuit of happiness:

- find good, even in the bad
- count your blessings
- connect with nature
- offer kindness
- follow your passions
- visualize success
- use your strengths
- connect with others
- be open to new experiences
- cultivate optimism
- don't compare yourself to others
- commit to meaningful goals
- practice religion and spirituality
- exercise
- eat well

Once you have your own unique list in mind, seek out life-giving experiences—fill your day with healthy thoughts, conversations, and actions.

Sharing

Research in the social sciences indicates that one of the best ways to extend and augment the positivity we feel is to tell others about our blessings. By recounting what has gone well, we leverage additional benefit from the interesting and meaningful experiences that come our way.

So let your friends know about the highly successful presentation you made. Make sure those closest to you are up-to-date on your most recent travel adventure. Find individuals interested in what you are doing and tell them about your successes. Spend time in conversations focusing on your most interesting and inspiring moments. By sharing positive feelings and experiences, you amplify and extend their impact.

One family I know has turned its evening meal into a time for expressing gratitude. Around the dinner table, each family member shares three things from that day that he or she is grateful for. This may be something as profound as freedom or as seemingly mundane as a good steak. This routine is an opportunity for each person to reflect on the blessings in his or her life and also learn what others find valuable and meaningful. As a result of this time together, they are more positive and more aware of the good in their day.

As you consider how you might add positivity to your day, rather than tackling everything at once, select the method you believe will work the best for you. By tailoring your approach to fit your particular needs and personality, you will make the process more enjoyable and improve the probability of success. Sonja Lyubomirsky, a well-respected happiness researcher, offers this tip: "… if there's any 'secret' to becoming happier, the secret is in establishing which happiness strategies suit you best." So pick the one you prefer—and then observe the impact.

The Positive Team

As a leader, you set the tone. Whether you are guiding a family, a small business, or a large multinational corporation, your mood and the way you interact with others influence the group's emotional climate.

Leaders who enable progress, offer respect, model positivity, and savor success create a positive environment—one that drives productivity.

Enable Progress

To foster positivity at work, make sure your teams have the resources and support necessary to reach their goals. Employees feel the best and have the greatest satisfaction when they succeed. The flipside is also true: The most difficult and negative workdays are the ones filled with frustrations and setbacks.

Theresa Amabile and Steven Kramer, in their research exploring the connection between what employees are feeling and their job performance, offer the following conclusion: "When we compared our study participants' best days (when they were most happy, had the most positive perceptions of the workplace, and were most intrinsically motivated) with their worst days, we found that the single most important differentiator was a sense of being able to make progress in their work. Achieving a goal, accomplishing a task, or solving a problem often evoked great pleasure and sometimes elation. Even making good progress toward such goals could elicit the same reactions."

There are a number of specific actions leaders can take to ensure that those they lead experience success. They can, for example:

- Provide direct, hands-on assistance. By helping with tasks critical to a project's success, a leader contributes to work completion and creates momentum.
- Make resources available. When employees are given what they need to complete an assigned task, they feel supported in their efforts.
- Set reasonable deadlines. Undue time pressure is a threat to morale, discouraging even the most dedicated employee.
- Offer constructive feedback. Input that focuses on appropriate corrective action is far more effective than critical appraisals of failings.
- Establish clear, specific, and measurable goals. Goals set expectations, focus effort, and provide needed direction.

When leaders set clear targets, provide adequate resources, offer assistance, and refrain from giving overly punitive feedback, they create a positive emotional climate and contribute to buy-in.

Offer Respect

As noted in the previous chapter, listening contributes to our capacity to build strong relational bonds. In addition, it's a simple, yet powerful, way to demonstrate our respect for others. When a subordinate is reporting to you, set aside whatever you are doing and pay close attention to what he is saying. Listen with your whole body—not with one ear as you multitask. This act communicates your interest in him, affirms his value, and enhances his self-esteem. When a colleague is describing her most recent parenting dilemma, make it a priority to stop what you are doing and focus on her story.

A friend, who is a partner in a large law firm, follows the rule: "The person in my office is the most important person in the world." When he meets with someone, regardless of the other person's status, he focuses his attention on that person. He won't allow himself to be interrupted by phone calls, text messages, e-mails, or other visitors. His phone is off, computer screen blank, and office door closed. This freely offered respect contributes to the positive emotional climate of his organization and deepens his connections with others.

Model Positivity

As a leader, how you approach your day influences how those around you approach theirs—your energy and your practices rub off. If you are upbeat and optimistic, others will be inclined to follow your lead. If you want teams that are known for their grit, set the tone; be the first one to arrive in the morning and the last one to leave at night. If your desire is to create a climate of mutual respect, model it in your interactions with peers and subordinates. This isn't to say you are responsible for how others think, feel, and act; but by establishing a positive tone you set the direction and make it more difficult for others to head in another, less positive one.

Savor Success

When a team you lead reaches an important milestone or finishes a challenging project, take time to celebrate before marching on to the next task. Focus on what went well and how each member contributed. Publicly praise individuals who exerted extra effort. By taking time to savor good outcomes, you add positivity to your team—a positivity that will promote engagement and improve future performance. Also, there is no need to wait until the end of a project to recognize a team's achievements. Make celebration a daily occurrence that is shared in the moment. The goal is to create a climate in which it's natural to talk about what is going well.

Consider the following exercise: For the next week or two begin meetings with the questions: "What is going well?" and "Why?" Ask team members to share what they are accomplishing. Then, encourage them to identify the reasons for their success. Was it extraordinary effort? Perhaps the gains were based on an innovative idea. Or maybe the achievements were the result of great teamwork—everyone doing what he or she does best. Focusing on the connection between actions and outcomes gives team members a sense of control, a belief they have a say in how things turn out. This boosts confidence and instills a sense of optimism.

Feelings are contagious. By enabling progress, offering respect, modeling positivity, and savoring success, leaders contribute to the spread of positivity within the teams they lead. This inspires investment and unlocks potential.

One Leader's Experience

Rob, a CEO with 30 years of organizational leadership experience, offers the following anecdote, inviting us to reflect on how we are perceived by others:

A few years ago I had a close friend who was diagnosed with a fatal form of cancer. When she passed away, I delivered the eulogy at her funeral. With this type of closure to our friendship, you can imagine my surprise when, six months later, I received a phone call with her name showing up on my

Caller ID. I remember being shocked at first, and then confused as I tried to imagine how she could be calling me. When I finally got the nerve to answer, it was her husband who was on the other end of the line. While I am sure you have already figured it out, he was using his wife's phone and her number was still in my contact list.

My reaction to seeing her name is probably more dramatic than most, but isn't it true we tend to respond emotionally when certain people call? You probably have individuals whose names evoke a very positive response and you are delighted to pick up the phone and talk to them. You likely also have others who cause you to frown and allow their calls to go directly to voicemail.

My question for you to ponder is this: What kind of reaction do people have when they see your name on their Caller ID? Do they smile when they see it because they know that this is going to be an enjoyable, motivational call, or do they frown?

As leaders we need to be intentional about connecting with others in a way that inspires a consistently positive response.

An Experiment

In this chapter, I have identified a number of activities designed to help you become a more positive leader and help the teams you lead develop a healthy emotional climate. A list of these activities is provided below.

As you review this list, consider the following exercise: First, identify the activities that are already part of your leadership skill set—ones you have already mastered. Next, read through the list a second time and find something new you would like to try. Select something that fits your personality and would be relatively easy to implement. Then, try it out on a daily basis for several days.

The Positive Leader:

- *Savoring*: Spend time reflecting on all that is good in your life.
- *Seeking*: Add an enjoyable activity to your schedule.
- *Sharing*: Tell others about your latest positive experience.

The Positive Team:

- *Enable Progress*: Ask your team how you can help them achieve success.
- *Offer Respect*: Take an interest in others by listening carefully.
- *Model Positivity*: Contribute to a healthy emotional climate by being positive.
- *Savor Success*: Begin team meetings by asking: "What is going well?" and "Why?"

Approach this exercise as an experiment. Change your behavior and observe the impact on the teams you lead—determine, from your experience, if emotions are indeed contagious. Does your positivity foster a positive emotional climate and is there a noticeable change in the engagement and persistence of the teams you lead?

KEY CONCEPTS

Feelings are contagious

We are influenced by the emotions of others. The mood on a particular day spreads from person to person.

Positivity drives productivity

Positive emotions inspire grit, which results in success. Individuals who are upbeat are more engaged and more willing to persist, even when the going gets tough.

HABIT

Conclusion: Habit

We Are What We Repeatedly Do

---

*Motivation is what gets you started.
Habit is what keeps you going.*

—Jim Ryun

Bill was standing next to his booth at a military technology show in Singapore when he and one of his partners noticed two sailors walking with purpose. "These guys are on a mission," Bill's partner observed. Then, to their surprise, rather than continuing on, the sailors stopped and queried, "Are you the MOBI guys?" Not knowing what to expect and with a good bit of apprehension, Bill answered, "Ah, yes we are." To which one of the sailors responded, "On our trip here, your device saved one of our buddies. He fell overboard and we turned around and fished him out of the water. Thanks! Thanks a lot!"

Bill Dull is a founding partner of BriarTek—a company that designs and manufactures specialty electronic devices to aid in the recovery of individuals who have gone missing. MOBI, *Man Overboard Identification*, is one of their product lines. When a sailor falls overboard, the MOBI system is activated, alerting the ship's crew and pinpointing the sailor's location so he or she is more easily rescued. Bill's company began as a serendipitous conversation and a drawing on the back of a napkin. Today, it's a successful and growing enterprise with a vision and mission focused on researching and developing life-saving electronic technology. At the time of this writing, 35 overboard sailors have been plucked from the sea with the help of the MOBI system.

I frequently wonder how life on this planet might change for the better if more people, like Bill, found their calling. What if more leaders developed their own capacities to the fullest? And what if, at the same time, they made it their highest priority to develop their LI and, as a result, inspire others to reach their potential? I am convinced that if this were to occur, the world would be a better place. Poverty, illness, and strife would decline. Our relationships would be stronger and we would experience more personal positivity and satisfaction. The teams, companies, and even the families we lead would all be more successful.

In this final chapter, you will find a strategy for boosting your LI.

The Person in the Mirror

As I suggest in the introduction, a leader's most important asset is the person in the mirror. LI is not only about bringing out the best in others; it's also about improving oneself. Leaders set the tone, leading first by example.

Below is an exercise, designed to help you develop habits that will contribute to your personal success and well-being:

- Spend a few minutes in the evening reflecting on the best parts of your day. How did you contribute to your growth and development? In your mind, rewind your life as if it were a video recording, and pause in order to recall specific situations in which you were at your best.
- Consider each of the antecedents of grit, success, and well-being described in this book. What did you do to …
  - use your *competencies* (strengths)?
  - increase your *optimism* and *confidence*?
  - add *meaning* and *passion* to your life?
  - boost your *energy* level?
  - offer *undivided attention* and strengthen your relationships?
  - maintain your *positivity*?

- Limit yourself to one or two specific situations, recalling them in detail:
  - Who was involved?
  - When during the day did it occur?
  - What exactly did you do to add to your success and well-being?
  - How did you feel?
- Over the next few days, as you reflect on what you are doing to build your capacities and reach your potential, what strengths do you observe in yourself? What are you already doing that is helping you reach your potential?
- Next, identify one new habit you would like to develop.
  - If you have difficulty identifying and selecting a new habit, review the suggestions described in this book. Appendix A, *Self-leadership*, summarizes these suggestions and references the pages where each is explained in more detail.
  - Another source for ideas is the high LI leaders in your life. What are these leaders doing to develop their own capacities and strengths? What can you learn from their example?
  - One final resource is *The Self-leadership Questionnaire* (see Appendix B). This questionnaire is designed to provide you with a global sense for how well you are doing with respect to the personal qualities identified in this book. Take a few minutes to fill it out and use what you learn about yourself to identify your current strengths and weaknesses.
- Once you have settled on a habit you wish to develop, find unique ways to express this new habit. Take every opportunity to try it out until it becomes automatic.

A Positive Climate (COME UP)

In addition to focusing on your personal growth, consider how you might develop a climate that brings out the best in others.

- Spend a few minutes at the end of your day reflecting on what you are already doing to help those around you flourish. In your mind, rewind the past 24 hours in order to recall specific interactions in which you inspired family, friends, or co-workers to reach their potential.

- As you recall the experiences of your day, consider each of the six characteristics of a positive climate described in this book. With respect to the individuals you lead, what did you do to …
  - empower them to use their *competencies*?
  - boost their *optimism* and *confidence*?
  - help them find *meaning* in or *passion* for what they do?
  - energize them?
  - strengthen their connection with others (*undivided attention*)?
  - add to their *positivity*?
- Limit your reflection to one or two interactions, recalling them in detail.
  - Who was involved?
  - When during the day did the interaction occur?
  - What exactly did you do to add to the positive climate?
  - How did you feel?
  - What was the impact on the person with whom you were interacting?
- Over the next few days, as you reflect on your LI, what strengths do you observe in yourself? What do you do well with respect to creating a climate that helps others succeed?
- After you have spent a few days contemplating what you are currently doing, identify one new leadership habit you would like to develop.
  - If you have difficulty identifying and selecting a new habit to enhance your LI, review the suggestions described in this book. Appendix C (*A Positive Climate: COME UP*) summarizes these suggestions and references the pages in the book where each is found.
  - Another source for ideas is the high LI leaders who have influenced you. As you consider their impact on your life, identify specifically what these leaders do that inspires you. Focus on their actions—their leadership habits that have affected you the most.

- A final resource is *The Leadership Intelligence Questionnaire* provided in Appendix D. This questionnaire is designed to be filled out by individuals who know you well enough to assess your capacity to create a climate that inspires competence, optimism & confidence, meaning & passion, energy, undivided attention, and positivity. It's an evaluation tool that provides you with input from others that you can use to identify your strengths and weakness.
- Once you have settled on a habit you wish to develop, find unique ways to express this new habit. Take every opportunity to try it out until it becomes automatic—part of your normal daily interactions with others.

As you read *Leadership Intelligence*, you were introduced to a positive approach to leadership. I hope you personally benefited and grew in your capacity to bring out the best in others. If that is the case, then this book has met its goal of helping leaders and those they lead invest in what matters most, succeed at the highest level, and, along the way, experience a profound sense of well-being.

APPENDICES

Appendix A
Self-leadership

In this book, I have identified and described a number of activities designed to contribute to your personal success and well-being. As a summary and review, these activities are listed below along with page numbers where you will find more detailed explanations.

Competence (pp. 33-35)

- Identify your competencies—the skills, knowledge, and characteristics that set you apart.
- Use your competencies on a regular basis—play life to your strengths.
- Develop your competencies—constantly strive to improve.

Optimism & Confidence (pp. 53-57)

- Cultivate optimism.
  - Be lenient about setbacks—accept responsibility and learn from mistakes, but don't be overly self-critical.
  - Appreciate the positive aspects of your current situation—what is good in your life right now and what can be learned from your current difficulties.
  - Focus on future possibilities and opportunities—expect good things to happen.
- Build confidence.
  - Mastery—success in past endeavors builds confidence for future ones.
  - Observation—observing others' successes builds confidence.
  - Encouragement—words of encouragement build confidence.
  - Well-being—feeling physically well builds confidence in every dimension of life.

Meaning & Passion (pp. 79-80)

- Envision your *best possible self*—visualize a future in which everything has gone as planned. You have reached all of your life goals.
- Imagine your *best possible d*ay—a day in which your time is spent doing what matters most.
- Do what you value and what you love—center your life on activities that will help you reach your potential.

Energy (pp. 104-105)

- Add autonomy to your day.
- Build positive connections with others.
- Take breaks.
- Exercise.
- Eat well.
- Get adequate sleep.

Undivided Attention (pp. 126-130)

- Listen well.
- Expect the best in others.
- Encourage those around you.
- Challenge others to reach their potential.

Positivity (pp. 145-148)

- Mindfully appreciate positive experiences (Savor).
- Engage in activities that elicit positive feelings (Seek).
- Tell others about your positive experiences (Share).

Appendix B
The Self-leadership Questionnaire

The Self-leadership Questionnaire assesses your personal strengths and weaknesses with respect to the qualities identified in this book (competence, optimism & confidence, meaning & passion, energy, undivided attention, and positivity).

Additional copies are available by clicking the "Download" tab at leadershipintelligencethebook.com.

The Self-leadership Questionnaire		
Instructions: Read each statement and indicate your level of agreement. Do not spend a great deal of time with any particular item; simply record your first impression. Circle 1 if you strongly disagree, circle 5 if you strongly agree, or circle a 2, 3, or 4 if you are somewhere between strong disagreement and strong agreement.		
1C. I spend most of my day doing things that I am good at.	Strongly Disagree	Strongly Agree
	1 2 3	4 5
2C. I am constantly striving to get better.	Strongly Disagree	Strongly Agree
	1 2 3	4 5
3C. I love to learn new things.	Strongly Disagree	Strongly Agree
	1 2 3	4 5
4C. I know my strengths well (what I am good at).	Strongly Disagree	Strongly Agree
	1 2 3	4 5
5O. I find the good, even in the midst of the toughest challenges.	Strongly Disagree	Strongly Agree
	1 2 3	4 5

The Self-leadership Questionnaire

6O. I expect to succeed.	Strongly Disagree Strongly Agree 1 2 3 4 5
7O. I can do most anything asked of me.	Strongly Disagree Strongly Agree 1 2 3 4 5
8O. I am good at what I do.	Strongly Disagree Strongly Agree 1 2 3 4 5
9M. I view my work as a calling—it's interesting and meaningful.	Strongly Disagree Strongly Agree 1 2 3 4 5
10M. I love what I do.	Strongly Disagree Strongly Agree 1 2 3 4 5
11M. I have a mission to fulfill and a vision for my life.	Strongly Disagree Strongly Agree 1 2 3 4 5
12M. I live each day in pursuit of what matters most.	Strongly Disagree Strongly Agree 1 2 3 4 5
13E. I get to choose how I spend my time.	Strongly Disagree Strongly Agree 1 2 3 4 5
14E. I take breaks during the day.	Strongly Disagree Strongly Agree 1 2 3 4 5
15E. I get enough sleep.	Strongly Disagree Strongly Agree 1 2 3 4 5
16E. I exercise regularly.	Strongly Disagree Strongly Agree 1 2 3 4 5

The Self-leadership Questionnaire

17U. I listen well.	Strongly Disagree	Strongly Agree
	1 2 3 4 5	
18U. I assume the best in others.	Strongly Disagree	Strongly Agree
	1 2 3 4 5	
19U. I care about others.	Strongly Disagree	Strongly Agree
	1 2 3 4 5	
20U. I want to see those around me succeed.	Strongly Disagree	Strongly Agree
	1 2 3 4 5	
21P. I am upbeat most of the time.	Strongly Disagree	Strongly Agree
	1 2 3 4 5	
22P. I savor all that is good and take the time to enjoy life.	Strongly Disagree	Strongly Agree
	1 2 3 4 5	
23P. I tell others about the good things that come my way.	Strongly Disagree	Strongly Agree
	1 2 3 4 5	
24P. I experience far more good than bad.	Strongly Disagree	Strongly Agree
	1 2 3 4 5	

Once you have completed the questionnaire, summarize your responses by following the instructions in the form provided below.

The Self-leadership Questionnaire Summary Form	Subtotals
Competence (sum of items 1C to 4C)	
Optimism & Confidence (sum of items 5O to 8O)	
Meaning & Passion (sum of items 9M to 12M)	
Energy (sum of items 13E to 16E)	
Undivided Attention (sum of items 17U to 20U)	
Positivity (sum of items 21P to 24P)	
TOTAL (sum of the subtotals)	

Your total score on this questionnaire will fall between 24 and 120, with 120 suggesting that, in general, you excel at self-leadership. Your subtotals on the individual characteristics will range from 4 to 20 (with 4 representing a weakness and 20 representing a strength). For example, if your score on undivided attention is a 20, this signifies an area in which you are doing well. Conversely, if your score on the competence dimension is a 5, this is an area where you may want to do some work.

Appendix C
A Positive Climate (COME UP)

In this book, I have identified and described a number of activities designed to help you create a positive climate that inspires competence, optimism & confidence, meaning & passion, energy, undivided attention, and positivity. As a summary and review, these activities are listed below along with page numbers where more detailed explanations are found.

Competence (pp. 36-37)

- Know team member competencies.
- Build teams based on needed competencies.
- Encourage the use of competencies.
- Strengthen current competencies.
- Develop new competencies.

Optimism & Confidence (pp. 57-60)

- Ensure Success—past success contributes to optimism and confidence.
- Think Positively—leaders who make positive interpretations of events in the life of a team add to that team's optimism and confidence.
- Encourage Others—words of encouragement are an important source of optimism and confidence.

Meaning & Passion (pp. 80-86)

- Define What's Important: Identify and emphasize the core values that guide decisions and actions.
- Set the Example: Model the values you want your teams to emulate.
- Create a Narrative: Help others understand the importance of their contribution and find meaning in what they do.

Energy (pp. 105-108)

- Conduct an energy audit.
- Design jobs and tasks so that they energize.
- Build positive relationships with team members.
- Offer support.

Undivided Attention (pp. 130-131)

- Model It: Set the example by relating well with others.
- Teach It: Help those you lead build high-quality relationships.
- Expect It: Make strong relational bonds the norm.
- Acknowledge It: Affirm positive interactions.

Positivity (pp. 148-151)

- Enable progress.
  - Provide adequate resources.
  - Offer to help.
  - Set reasonable deadlines.
  - Provide appropriate, focused feedback without undue negativity.
  - Set clear, specific, and measurable goals.
- Offer respect.
  - Listen.
  - Take an active interest in others.
- Model Positivity.
- Savor Success.
  - Celebrate accomplishments.
  - Spend time reflecting on what is going well.

Appendix D
The Leadership Intelligence Questionnaire

The Leadership Intelligence Questionnaire is designed to be filled out by individuals who know you well and can evaluate your capacity to lead.

Give this questionnaire to several subordinates and peers who can assess your LI. To guarantee anonymity, you may wish to have a colleague distribute, score, and summarize the results for you. Anonymous, broad-based feedback will assure candor and give you the most accurate insight into your overall capacity to bring out the best in others.

Additional copies are available by clicking the "Download" tab at leadershipintelligencethebook.com.

The Leadership Intelligence Questionnaire		
Instructions: The individual you are evaluating is interested in growing his or her capacity to lead. This leader wants to know how he or she is doing with respect to helping you reach your potential. Based on your experience with him or her, read each item and indicate your level of agreement. Do not spend a great deal of time with any particular item; simply record your first impression. Circle 1 if you strongly disagree, circle 5 if you strongly agree, or circle a 2, 3, or 4 if you are somewhere between strong disagreement and strong agreement.		
1C. This leader encourages me to use my strengths.	Strongly Disagree	Strongly Agree
	1 2 3 4 5	
2C. This leader values my skill and knowledge.	Strongly Disagree	Strongly Agree
	1 2 3 4 5	
3C. This leader provides helpful feedback and instruction that enables me to improve.	Strongly Disagree	Strongly Agree
	1 2 3 4 5	

The Leadership Intelligence Questionnaire

4C. This leader knows my strengths—what I bring to the table.	Strongly Disagree 1 2 3 4 5 Strongly Agree
5O. This leader believes in my ability to get the job done.	Strongly Disagree 1 2 3 4 5 Strongly Agree
6O. This leader frames difficulties in the best possible light, looking for the benefit in even the most challenging experience.	Strongly Disagree 1 2 3 4 5 Strongly Agree
7O. This leader is in my corner, ready to do whatever it takes to help me succeed.	Strongly Disagree 1 2 3 4 5 Strongly Agree
8O. This leader isn't punitive or blaming when things don't go as planned.	Strongly Disagree 1 2 3 4 5 Strongly Agree
9M. This leader helps me find meaning in what I do.	Strongly Disagree 1 2 3 4 5 Strongly Agree
10M. This leader makes sure that I know my team's key values—what's important.	Strongly Disagree 1 2 3 4 5 Strongly Agree
11M. This leader consistently models important values.	Strongly Disagree 1 2 3 4 5 Strongly Agree
12M. This leader affirms my contribution.	Strongly Disagree 1 2 3 4 5 Strongly Agree
13E. This leader gives me autonomy—I'm not micromanaged.	Strongly Disagree 1 2 3 4 5 Strongly Agree
14E. This leader lets me try new things.	Strongly Disagree 1 2 3 4 5 Strongly Agree

Appendix D The Leadership Intelligence Questionnaire | 175

The Leadership Intelligence Questionnaire		
15E. This leader challenges me.	Strongly Disagree	Strongly Agree
	1 2 3	4 5
16E. This leader trusts me.	Strongly Disagree	Strongly Agree
	1 2 3	4 5
17U. This leader relates well with others.	Strongly Disagree	Strongly Agree
	1 2 3	4 5
18U. This leader expects team members to get along.	Strongly Disagree	Strongly Agree
	1 2 3	4 5
19U. This leader prohibits incivility.	Strongly Disagree	Strongly Agree
	1 2 3	4 5
20U. This leader values cooperation over competition.	Strongly Disagree	Strongly Agree
	1 2 3	4 5
21P. This leader is upbeat most of the time.	Strongly Disagree	Strongly Agree
	1 2 3	4 5
22P. This leader helps me make progress toward important goals.	Strongly Disagree	Strongly Agree
	1 2 3	4 5
23P. This leader clearly demonstrates respect for me.	Strongly Disagree	Strongly Agree
	1 2 3	4 5
24P. This leader acknowledges and celebrates my accomplishments.	Strongly Disagree	Strongly Agree
	1 2 3	4 5

After the questionnaire is returned to you, summarize the results by following the instructions in the form provided below.

The Leadership Intelligence Questionnaire Summary Form	Subtotals
Competence (sum of items 1C to 4C)	
Optimism & Confidence (sum of items 5O to 8O)	
Meaning & Passion (sum of items 9M to 12M)	
Energy (sum of items 13E to 16E)	
Undivided Attention (sum of items 17U to 20U)	
Positivity (sum of items 21P to 24P)	
TOTAL (sum of the subtotal scores)	

Your total score on this questionnaire will fall between 24 and 120, with 120 suggesting you excel at creating a climate that brings out the best in others (high LI). Your subtotals on the individual climate characteristics will range from 4 to 20 with 4 representing a weakness and 20 representing a strength. For example, if your score on energy is a 20, this signifies an area in which you are doing well. Conversely, if your score on the meaning & passion dimension is a 5, this is an area where you may want to do some work.

Acknowledgements

If it takes a village to raise a child, then a small city is required to write a book. From the very first word, *Leadership Intelligence* was influenced by many—a few I knew well, but most I met along the way.

I am indebted to the scholars whose research forms the scaffolding from which this book is built. Many more could be acknowledged, but core ideas were borrowed from Martin Seligman, Christopher Peterson, Sonja Lyubomirsky, Angela Duckworth, Adam Grant, K. Anders Ericsson, Richard Ryan, Edward Deci, Amy Wrzesniewski, Jane Dutton, Gregory Berns, and Kennon Sheldon. Through their research, these investigators help us understand more fully how we can extract the most from each day and help those we lead do the same.

Then, there are the high LI leaders I have the privilege of knowing. These leaders graciously and generously shared their time and insights with me. Each of them has mastered the art of helping others thrive. To Mike Tooley, Erica Thomas, Tom Ewald, Doug Felton, Graham Carlos, Aaron Brockett, Rob Parker, Sue Bondurant, Kenneth Gwirtz, Jamie Lee, Bill Dull, David Estes, and Jeff McClintic, I offer a heartfelt thank you. Their leadership inspires me and countless others who benefit from their LI.

I couldn't be more grateful for Judy Keene, editor extraordinaire. Her careful eye sees all. She patiently improved the text, making the revision process a pleasure. Every page is its own testimony to her skill and capacity to perfect a manuscript.

Finally, and of primary importance, none of this would be possible without the support of family. My wife Lynette, son Alex, daughter-in-law Sarah, grandson Will, daughter Hayleigh, and son-in-law Adam are my greatest inspiration. With understanding and patience, they encouraged me and freely granted me the countless hours required to complete this project. Their LI is off the charts, making me—and everyone they meet—better.

Notes & References

Preface

i   **Andrew Carnegie:** Nasaw, D. (2006). *Andrew Carnegie*. New York: The Penguin Press. Carnegie, A. (1889). Wealth. *The North American Review,* 148(391), 653-664. http://www.nytimes.com/learning/gen-eral/onthisday/bday/1125.html.

i   **nearly $169 billion in 2014 dollars:** To calculate Carnegie's wealth in 2014 dollars, I used the calculator provided on the website, *MeasuringWorth.com* (http://www.measuringworth.com/uscompare/).

i   **... *I will answer your question by saying* ...:** The Carnegie quote is from page 204 in Napoleon, H. (2010). *What Would Napoleon Hill Do?* Los Angeles: Highroads Media, Inc.

ii   **"If I have seen a little further, ...":** Sir Isaac Newton's quote is from http://www.phrases.org.uk/meanings/268025.html.

iii   **require in order to thrive in all aspects of life:** Seligman, M.E.P. (2011). *Flourish: A Visionary New Understanding of Happiness and Well-Being*. New York: Free Press. Peterson, C. (2006). *A Primer in Positive Psychology*. Oxford: Oxford University Press.

Introduction: Grit

3   *Everyone knows on any given day* ...: James, W. (1907). The energies of men. *Science,* 25(635), 321–332.

3   **Its graduates include a pantheon of great military, government, and business leaders:** Notable leaders who trained at West Point Military Academy include: Jefferson Davis (President of the Confederate States of America); Robert E. Lee (General in Chief, Confederate Armies); Ulysses S. Grant (18th President of the United States); Douglas MacArthur (Supreme Commander of the Pacific, 1941-1945); Dwight D. Eisenhower (34th President of the United States); John G. Hayes (Former President of Coca-Cola Bottling Co.); Frank Borman (Astronaut and President of Eastern Airlines); Mike Krzyzewski (Duke University Head Men's Basketball Coach and U.S. Men's Olympic Basketball Head Coach); George S. Patton, Jr. (Commander of the 3rd Army European Theater, 1944-1945); William T. Seawell (Former Chairman of the Board and Chief Executive Officer, Pan Am World Airways); Reuben Pomerantz (Former President, Holiday Inns of America); Randolph Araskog (President and Chairman of ITT); Peter Dawkins (Chairman and CEO Primerica); James V. Kimsey (Founding Chairman of America on Line).

4   **grit:** Duckworth, A.L., Peterson, C., Matthews, M.D., & Kelly, D.R. (2007). Grit: Perseverance and passion for long-term goals. *Journal of Personality and Social Psychology,* 92(6), 1087-1101.

4   **there is not a single documented case of a chess player reaching the grandmaster level without a decade of intense practice:** Simon, H.A., & Chase, W.G. (1973). Skill in chess. *American Scientist,* 61(4), 394-403.

4   **Scientists and writers often toil for years before they produce their best work.**: A study of scientists and writers suggests that there is about a 10-year interval between their first work and their greatest work. See Raskin, E. (1936). Comparison of scientific and literary ability: A biographical study of eminent scientists and men of letters of the nineteenth century. *The Journal of Abnormal and Social Psychology*, 31(1), 20-35.

5   **the top-level violinists had practiced an average of more than 10,000 hours**: Ericsson, K. A., Krampe, R.T., & Tesch-Romer, C. (1993). The role of deliberate practice in the acquisition of expert performance. *Psychological Review*, 100(3), 363-406.

5   **grandmaster chess players spend between 10,000 and 50,000 hours "staring at chess positions"**: The comparison of grandmaster chess players' practice time to that of less-accomplished players is found in Simon, H. A., & Chase, W. G. (1973). Skill in chess. *American Scientist*, 61(4), 394-403.

6   **"Give me a dozen healthy infants ..."**: See p. 82 in Watson, J. B. (1930). Behaviorism (Revised Edition). Chicago: University of Chicago Press.

7   **incentives have been shown to decrease motivation and grit**: Murayama, K., Matsumoto, M., Izuma, K., & Matsumoto, K. (2010). Neural basis of the undermining effect of monetary reward on intrinsic motivation. *Proceedings of the National Academy of Sciences*, 107(49), 20911-20916. Pink, D.H. (2009) *Drive: The Surprising Truth About What Motivates Us.* New York: Penguin Group.

7   **dampen one's desire to learn, explore, and achieve**: Deci, E.L., Koestner, R., & Ryan R.M. (1999). A meta-analytic review of experiments examining the effects of extrinsic rewards on intrinsic motivation, *Psychological Bulletin*, 125(6), 627-668.

7   **Individuals engaged because they genuinely enjoy what they are doing receive better grades, are more creative, are more productive in their jobs, and have healthier lifestyles.**: Black, A. E., & Deci, E. L. (2000). The effects of instructors' autonomy support and students' autonomous motivation on learning organic chemistry: A self-determination theory perspective. *Science Education*, 84(6), 740–756. Koestner, R., Ryan, R.M., Bernieri, F., & Holt, K. (1984). Setting limits on children's behavior: The differential effects of controlling vs. informational styles on intrinsic motivation and creativity. *Journal of Personality*, 52(3), 233–248. Fernet, C., Guay, F., & Senecal, C. (2004). Adjusting to job demands: The role of work self-determination and job control in predicting burnout. *Journal of Vocational Behavior*, 65(1), 39–56. Pelletier, L.G., Fortier, M.S., Vallerand, R.J., & Briere, N.M. (2001). Associations among perceived autonomy support, forms of self-regulation, and persistence: A prospective study. *Motivation and Emotion*, 25(4), 279–306.

8   **a keynote address**: For the full text of this address see *http://www.ppc.sas.upenn.edu/aparep98.htm*.

8   **"Positive psychology is the scientific study of what goes right in life, ..."**: See p. 4 in Peterson, C. (2006). *A Primer in Positive Psychology*. Oxford: Oxford University Press.

10 **Tasks and projects that utilize a person's strengths naturally engender persistent engagement.**: Rawls, J. (1971). *A Theory of Justice.* Cambridge, MA: Harvard University Press. Ryan, R.M., & Deci, E.L. (2000). Self-determination theory and the facilitation of intrinsic motivation, social development, and well-being. *American Psychologist*, 55(1), 68-78.

10 **they gave up easily because they had lost confidence**: Jacobs, B., Prentice-Dunn, S., & Rogers, R.W. (1984). Understanding persistence: An interface of Control Theory and Self-Efficacy Theory. *Basic and Applied Social Psychology*, 5(4), 333-347.

11	residents who view their career as a means for expressing important values achieve more, find greater satisfaction in what they do, and ultimately experience a greater sense of well-being: Wrzesniewski, A. (2012). Callings. In K.S. Cameron & G.M. Spreitzer (Eds.), *The Oxford Handbook of Positive Organizational Scholarship* (45-55). Oxford: Oxford University Press.
12	**Individuals invigorated by what they do perform better and experience less burnout.**: Spreitzer, G., & Porath, C. (2012). Creating sustainable performance: If you give your employees the chance to learn and grow, they'll thrive—and so will your organization. *Harvard Business Review*, 90(1/2), 92-99.
12	**Interactions characterized by trust and respect add to the vitality that is experienced:** Dutton, J.E. (2003). *Energize Your Workplace: How to Create and Sustain High-Quality Connections at Work*. San Francisco: Jossey-Bass.
14	**companies with a positive emotional climate excelled in all areas of performance that were measured:** Ozcelik, H., Langton, N., & Aldrich, H. (2008). Doing well and doing good: The relationship between leadership practices that facilitate a positive emotional climate and organizational performance. *Journal of Managerial Psychology*, 23(2), 186-203.
14	**members of the more upbeat teams were evaluated more favorably by superiors, peers, and subordinates:** Losada, M., & Heaphy, E. (2004). The role of positivity and connectivity in the performance of business teams: A nonlinear dynamics model. *American Behavioral Scientist*, 47(6), 740-765.
14	**the connection between goals, effort, success, and well-being:** Sheldon, K.M., & Elliot, A.J. (1999). Goal striving, need satisfaction, and longitudinal well-being: The self-concordance model. *Journal of Personality and Social Psychology*, 76(3), 482-497.
15	**Happiness and fulfillment are often found in the determined pursuit of what one cares about most.:** Ben-Shahar, T. (2007). *Happier: Learn the Secrets of Daily Joy and Lasting Fulfillment*. New York: McGraw-Hill. Lyubomirsky, S. (2007). *The How of Happiness: A Scientific Approach to Getting the Life You Want*. New York: The Penguin Press.

One: Competence

25	**… the master lever is getting each person to play to his strengths:** Buckingham, M. (2007). *Go Put Your Strengths to Work: 6 Powerful Steps to Achieve Outstanding Performance*. New York: The Free Press.
27	**"The Aristotelian Principle states …":** See p. 414 in Rawls, J. (1971). *A Theory of Justice*. Cambridge, MA: Harvard University Press.
27	**Mastery is its own reward.:** White, R.W. (1959). Motivation reconsidered: The concept of competence. *Psychological Review*, 66(5), 297-333.
27	**children ages six to the onset of puberty who develop a sense of competence fare better than those who fail to do so:** Erikson, E.H. (1963). *Childhood and Society* (2nd Ed.). New York: W.W. Norton & Co.
27	**competence a basic human need:** Ryan, R.M., & Deci, E.L. (2000). Self-determination theory and the facilitation of intrinsic motivation, social development, and well-being. *American Psychologist*, 55(1), 68-78.
28	**"… this region, which may hold the key to satisfaction, thrives on challenge and novelty.":** See p. xi in Burns, G. (2005). *Satisfaction: The Science of Finding True Fulfillment*. New York: Henry Holt and Co.

29 **daily fluctuations in well-being were closely tied to competence:** Sheldon, K.M., Ryan, R., & Reis, H. T. (1996). What makes for a good day? Competence and autonomy in the day and in the person. *Personality and Social Psychology Bulletin*, 22(12), 1270-1279.

29 **the role of strengths (competencies) in improving the performance of individuals and organizations:** Rath, T. (2007). *Strengths Finder 2.0*. New York: Gallup Press.

29 **an 11 percent increase in sales:** *http://businessjournal.gallup.com/con-tent/13960/how-marriott-vacation-club-international-engages-talent.aspx*.

29 **lower turnover, greater productivity, and higher customer satisfaction scores:** Buckingham, M., Clifton, D.O. (2001). *Now, Discover Your Strengths*. New York: The Free Press. Harter, J.K., Schmidt, F.L., & Hayes, T.L. (2002). Business-unit-level relationship between employee satisfaction, employee engagement, and business outcomes: A meta-analysis. *Journal of Applied Psychology*, 87(2), 268-279.

29 *Groundhog Day:* Ramis, H. (Director). (1993). *Groundhog Day. Culver City, California*: Columbia Pictures.

30 **experience alone does not inevitably result in better performance:** Camerer, C.F., & Johnson, E.J. (1991). The process-performance paradox in expert judgment: How can experts know so much and predict so badly? In K.A. Ericsson & J. Smith (Eds.), *Toward a General Theory of Expertise: Prospects and Limits* (pp. 195-217). Cambridge: Cambridge University Press.

30 **in some situations less-experienced employees perform better:** Sengupta, K., Abdel-Hamid, T.K., & Van Wassenhove, L.N. (2008). The experience trap. *Harvard Business Review*, 86(2), 94-101.

31 **"… physicians who have been in practice…":** See p. 269 in Choudhry, N.K., Fletcher, R.H., & Soumerai, S.B. (2005). Systematic review: The relationship between clinical experience and quality of health care. *Annals of Internal Medicine,* 142(4), 260-273.

31 **mental health professionals' clinical performance:** Garb, H.N. (1989). Clinical judgment, clinical training, and professional experience. *Psychology Bulletin*, 105(3), 387-396.

31 **less experienced psychiatrists did just as well as the more experienced ones:** Kendell, R.E. (1973). Psychiatric diagnoses: A study of how they are made. *British Journal of Psychiatry*, 122, 437-445.

31 **psychiatry interns had the same diagnostic accuracy as ward secretaries:** Levenberg, S.B. (1975). Professional training, psychodiagnostic skill, and kinetic family drawings. *Journal of Personality Assessment*, 39(4), 389-393.

31 *deliberate practice*: Ericsson, K.A. (2004). Deliberate practice and the acquisition and maintenance of expert performance in medicine and related domains. *Academic Medicine*, 79(10 Suppl), S70-S81.

32 **they remembered 28.7 words:** Kliegl, R., Smith, J., & Baltes, P.B. (1989). Testing-the-limits and the study of adult age differences in cognitive plasticity of a mnemonic skill. *Developmental Psychology*, 25(2), 247-256.

32 **"In the absence of adequate feedback, …":** See p. 367 in Ericsson, K.A., Krampe, R.T., & Tesch-Romer, C. (1993). The role of deliberate practice in the acquisition of expert performance. *Psychological Review,* 100(3), 363-406.

32 **tutored students performed better:** Bloom, B.S. (1984). The 2 sigma problem: The search for methods of group instruction as effective as one-to-one tutoring. *Educational Researcher*, 13(6), 4-16.

33 **Vince Lombardi:** Vince Lombardi was the coach of the Green Bay Packers during the 1960s, when the Packers won three consecutive league championships and a total of five championships in a seven-year span.

33 **Leader Competencies:** This approach to identifying and leveraging competencies is based on input from several sources, including: Roberts, L.M., Spreitzer, G., Dutton, J., Quinn, R., Heaphy, E., & Barker, B. (2005). How to PLAY to your strengths. *Harvard Business Review*, 83(1), 74-80. Asplund, J., & Blacksmith, N. (2012). Productivity through strengths. In K.S. Cameron & G.M. Spreitzer (Eds.), *The Oxford Handbook of Positive Organizational Scholarship* (pp. 353-365). Oxford: Oxford University Press. Peterson, C. (2006). *A Primer in Positive Psychology.* Oxford: Oxford University Press.

33 **strengths:** Buckingham, M. (2007). *Go Put Your Strengths to Work.* New York: Free Press.

34 **character strengths:** See pp. 142-146 in Peterson, C. (2006). *A Primer in Positive Psychology*, Oxford: Oxford University Press.

34 **take this a step further:** In addition to Peterson's list, another source for identifying your personal character strengths is a survey developed by Donald Clifton and researchers associated with the Gallup organization (*Clifton StrengthsFinder*). This survey focuses on talents (strengths). Its developers define a talent as a preferred way of thinking, feeling, or behaving that, when combined with skill, knowledge, and hard work, results in a competency or strength. The survey identifies 34 talents including: communication, empathy, learner, positivity, and strategic. A complete list of the talents along with descriptions and ways to understand and apply them is available in Tom Rath's book *Strengths Finder 2.0.* Peruse this list and the accompanying descriptions to determine which ones best fit with your perception of yourself. Which of these talents do you use on a regular basis? Which ones are central to your identity? Also, if you wish, there is an online version of the survey (StrengthsFinder.com). An access code, provided in the back of Rath's book, is required to take the survey. After you have taken the survey, you will receive a list of your top five strengths, definitions of your strengths, and an action plan to implement them.

36 **only 1 percent of their employees disengaged:** See Rath, T. (2007). *Strengths Finder 2.0* New York: Gallup Press. Rath, T., & Clifton, D.O. (2009). *How Full Is Your Bucket? (Expanded Anniversary Edition)* New York: Gallup Press.

37 **an inherent satisfaction in taking on new challenges:** Burns, G. (2005). *Satisfaction: The Science of Finding True Fulfillment.* New York: Henry Holt and Co.

Two: Optimism & Confidence

43 *The mind is its own place*: See p. 11 (Book I—Lines 254-255) in Milton, J. (2004). *Paradise Lost* (Oxford World's Classics). Oxford: Oxford University Press.

44 **the connection between optimism, workplace productivity, and employee retention in a group of insurance agents:** Seligman, M.E., & Schulman, P. (1986). Explanatory style as a predictor of productivity and quitting among life insurance sales agents. *Journal of Personality and Social Psychology*, 50(4), 832-838.

44 **we are active shapers of our world:** Maddux, J.E. (2005). Self-Efficacy: the power of believing you can. In C.R. Snyder & S.J. Lopez (Eds.), *Handbook of Positive Psychology*, (pp. 277-287). Oxford: Oxford University Press.

44 **our minds give us the capacity to be active, choosing agents in life:** Bandura, A. (2001). Social cognitive theory: An agentic perspective. *Annual Review of Psychology*, 52, 1-26.

45   **They anticipate their efforts will be rewarded with achievement and success.:** Scheier, M.F., & Carver, C.S. (1992). Effects of optimism on psychological and physical well-being: Theoretical overview and empirical update. *Cognitive Therapy and Research*, 16(2), 201-228.

45   **This perspective is a source of motivation:** Carver, C.S., Scheier, M.F., Miller, C.J., & Fulford, D. (2009). Optimism. In S. J. Lopez & C.R. Snyder (Eds.), *The Oxford Handbook of Positive Psychology,* (pp. 303-312). Oxford: Oxford University Press.

45   **optimists offer positive explanations for the circumstances they encounter:** Luthans, F., Youssef, C.M., & Avolio, B.J. (2007). *Psychological Capital: Developing the Human Competitive Edge.* Oxford: Oxford University Press.

45   **Optimists have characteristic ways of explaining setbacks:** Peterson, C., & Steen, T.A. (2005). Optimistic Explanatory Style. C.R. Snyder & S.J. Lopez (Eds.), *Handbook of Positive Psychology* (pp. 244-256). Oxford: Oxford University Press.

46   **When pessimists have negative experiences, they tend to think ...:** Peterson, C., & Steen, T.A. (2005). Optimistic Explanatory Style. C.R. Snyder & S.J. Lopez (Eds.), *Handbook of Positive Psychology* (pp. 244-256). Oxford: Oxford University Press.

47   **Employees who expect the best are more productive, more satisfied with their jobs, and less likely to quit.:** Luthans, F., Avery, J.B., Clapp-Smith, R., & Li, W. (2008). More evidence on the value of Chinese workers' psychological capital: A potentially unlimited competitive resource? *The International Journal of Human Resource Management*, 19(5), 818-827. Luthans, F., Avolio, B.J., Avey, J.B., & Norman, S.M. (2007). Positive psychological capital: Measurement and relationship with performance and job satisfaction. *Personnel Psychology*, 60, 541-572. Avey, J.B., Luthans, F., & Jensen, S.M. (2009). Psychological capital: A positive resource for combating stress and turnover. *Human Resources Management*, 48(5), 677-693.

47   **Optimistic employees are more likely to work well with others and are more committed to the organizations they serve.:** See Avey, J.B., Luthans, F., & Youssef, C.M. (2010). The additive value of positive psychological capital in predicting work attitudes and behaviors. *Journal of Management*, 36, 430-452., Luthans, F., Norman, S.M., Avolio, B.J., & Avey, J.B. (2008). The mediating role of psychological capital in the supportive organizational climate-employee performance relationship. *Journal of Organizational Behavior*, 29(2), 219-238.

48   **Pessimists, on the other hand, take a very different approach to the challenges they face:** Nes, L.S., & Segerstrom, S.C. (2006). Dispositional optimism and coping: A meta-analytic review. *Personality and Social Psychology Review, 10(3), 235-251.*

48   **"In general, optimists tend to use more problem-focused coping strategies ...":** See p. 237 in Carver, C.S., & Scheier, M.F. (2005). Optimism. In C.R. Snyder & S.J. Lopez (Eds.), *Handbook of Positive Psychology* (pp. 231-243). Oxford, UK: Oxford University Press.

48   **The graduates who offered pessimistic responses to these questions had the most health problems:** Peterson, C., Seligman, M.E., Vaillant, G.E. (1988). Pessimistic explanatory style is a risk factor for physical illness: A thirty-five-year longitudinal study. *Journal of Personality and Social Psychology*, 55(1), 23-27.

48 **The health benefits of optimism are not limited to Harvard graduates.:** Wrosch, C., & Scheier, M.F. (2003). Personality and quality of life: The importance of optimism and goal adjustment. *Quality of Life Research*, 12(Suppl. 1), 59-72. Scheier, M.F., Matthews, K.A., Owens, J.F., Magovern, G.J. Sr., Lefebvre, R.C., Abbott, R.A., & Carver, C.S., (1989). Dispositional optimism and recovery from coronary artery bypass surgery: The beneficial effects on physical and psychological well-being. *Journal of Personality and Social Psychology*, 57(6), 1024-1040. Marshall, G.N., & Lang, E.L. (1990). Optimism, self-mastery, and symptoms of depression in women professionals. *Journal of Personality and Social Psychology*, 59(1), 132-139. Kubzansky, L.D., Sparrow, D., Vokonas, P., & Kawachi, I. (2001) Is the glass half empty or half full? A prospective study of optimism and coronary heart disease in the normative aging study. *Psychosomatic Medicine*, 63(9), 910-916. Scheier, M.F., & Carver, C.S. (1992). Effects of optimism on psychological and physical well-being: Theoretical overview and empirical update. *Cognitive Therapy and Research*, 16(2), 201-228.

49 **Optimism has also been linked to longevity.:** Giltay, E.J., Geleijnse, J.M., Zitman, F.G., Hoekstra, T., & Schouten, E.G. (2004). Dispositional Optimism and all-cause and cardiovascular mortality in a prospective cohort of elderly Dutch men and women. *Archives of General Psychiatry*, 61(11), 1126-1135.

49 **players with optimistic quotes lived longer than those whose quotes were pessimistic:** Peterson, C., & Seligman, M.E.P. (1987). Explanatory style and illness. *Journal of Personality*, 55(2). 237-265.

49 **self-efficacy:** Bandura, A. (1977). Self-efficacy: Toward a unifying theory of behavior change. *Psychology Review*, 84(2), 191-215.

49 **focuses on beliefs rather than skills:** Bandura, A. (1982). Self-efficacy mechanism in human agency. *American Psychologist*, 37(2), 122-147.

50 **missed fewer days of work and were on time more often:** McDonald, T., & Siegall, M. (1992). The effects of technological self-efficacy and job focus on job performance, attitudes, and withdrawal behaviors. *The Journal of Psychology*, 126(5), 465-475.

50 **confidence contributes to creativity and leadership ability:** Tierney, P., & Farmer, S.M. (2002). Creative self-efficacy: Its potential antecedents and relationship to creative performance. *Academy of Management Journal*, 45(6), 1137-1148. Chemers, M.M., Watson, C.B., & May, S.T. (2000). Dispositional affect and leadership effectiveness: A comparison of self-esteem, optimism, and efficacy. *Personality and Social Psychology Bulletin*, 26(3), 267-277. Judge, T.A., & Bono, J.E. (2001). Relationship of core self-evaluation traits—self-esteem, generalized self-efficacy, locus of control, and emotional stability—with job satisfaction and job performance: A meta-analysis. *Journal of Applied Psychology*, 86(1), 80-92.

50 **more persistent when faced with difficult tasks:** Jacobs, B., Prentice-Dunn, S., & Rogers, R.W. (1984). Understanding persistence: An interface of control theory and self-efficacy theory. *Basic and Applied Social Psychology*, 5(4), 333-347.

50 **confidence contributes more to work performance than goal setting or job satisfaction:** Stajkovic, A.D., & Luthans, F. (1998). Self-efficacy and work-related performance: A meta-analysis. *Psychological Bulletin*, 124(2), 240-261; See p. 42 in Luthans, F., Youssef, C.M., & Avolio, B.J. (2007). *Psychological Capital: Developing the Human Competitive Edge*. Oxford: Oxford University Press.

50　**confident individuals adapt better to illness:** Paukert, A.L., Pettit, J.W., Kunik, M.E., Wilson, N., Novy, D.M., Rhoades, H.M., Greisinger, A.J., Wehmanen, O.A., & Stanley, M.A. (2010). The roles of social support and self-efficacy in physical health's impact on depressive and anxiety symptoms in older adults. *Journal of Clinical Psychology in Medical Settings,* 17(4), 387-400.

50　**patients who believed they could cope well with their disease:** Brekke, M., & Kvien, T.K. (2001). Self-efficacy and health status in rheumatoid arthritis: A two-year longitudinal observational study. *Rheumatology,* 40(4), 387-392.

51　**in patients with heart disease, those who doubted their ability to deal with their illness experienced more problematic symptoms:** Sarkar, U., Ali, S., & Whooley, M.A. (2007). Self-efficacy and health status in patients with coronary heart disease: Finding from the heart and soul study. *Psychosomatic Medicine,* 69(4), 306-312.

51　**Confidence has also been shown to benefit individuals suffering with diabetes, cancer, and chronic pain.:** Sarkar, U., Fisher, L., & Schillinger, D. (2006). Is self-efficacy associated with diabetes self-management across race/ethnicity and health literacy? *Diabetes Care,* 29(4), 823-829. Salbach, N.M., Mayo, N.E., Robichaud-Ekstrand, S., Hanley, J.A., Richards, C.L., & Wood-Dauphinee, S. (2006). Balance self-efficacy and its relevance to physical function and perceived health status after stroke. *Archives of Physical Medicine and Rehabilitation,* 87(3), 364-370. Manne, S.L., Ostroff, J.S., Norton, T.R., Fox, K., Grana, G., & Goldstein, L. (2006). Cancer-specific self-efficacy and psychosocial functional adaptation to early stage breast cancer. *Annals of Behavioral Medicine,* 31(2), 145-154. Arnstein, P., Wells-Federman, C., & Caudill, M. (2001). The effect of an integrated cognitive-behavioral pain management program on pain intensity, self-efficacy beliefs and depression in chronic pain patients on completion and one year later. *Pain Medicine,* 2(3), 238-239.

51　**more successful when it comes to smoking cessation, weight control, and exercise maintenance:** Strecher, V.J., McEvoy, B., Becker, M.H., & Rosenstock, I.M. (1986). The role of self-efficacy in achieving health behavior change. *Health Education Quarterly,* 13(1), 73-92.

51　**In a study of college students, a link was found between self-assurance and an increased likelihood of engaging in positive health-related activities:** Jackson, E.S., Tucker, C.M., & Herman, K.C. (2007). Health value, perceived social support, and health self-efficacy as factors in a health-promoting lifestyle. *Journal of American College of Health,* 56(1), 69-74.

52　**Isn't there a downside to positive thinking:** Weinstein, N.D. (1989). Optimistic biases about personal risk. *Science,* 246(4935), 1232-1233.

52　**it is not without risk:** Peterson, C. (2000). The future of optimism. *American Psychologist,* 55(1), 44-55.

52　**a risk that positive thinking will actually result in decreased performance:** Vancouver, J.B., Thompson, C.M., Tischner, E.C., & Putka, D.J. (2002). Two studies examining the negative effect of self-efficacy on performance. *Journal of Applied Psychology,* 87(3), 506-516.

52　**optimism and confidence must be grounded in reality:** See pp. 126-128 in Peterson, C. (2006). *A Primer in Positive Psychology.* Oxford: Oxford University Press.

52　**"Realistic optimism relies on regular reality checks …":** See p. 257 in Schneider, S.L. (2001). In search of realistic optimism: Meaning, knowledge, and warm fuzziness. *American Psychologist,* 56(3), 250-263.

53　**flexible in your use of optimism and confidence:** Seligman, M.E.P. (1990). *Learned Optimism: How to Change Your Mind and Your Life.* New York: Knopf.

53　**when your actions have a direct influence on the results:** Peterson, C. (2000). The future of optimism. *American Psychologist,* 55(1), 44-55.

53 **"It's going to last forever," "It's going to undermine everything," and "It's all my fault.":** Peterson, C., & Steen, T. A. (2005). Optimistic explanatory style. C.R. Snyder & S.J. Lopez (Eds.), *Handbook of Positive Psychology* (pp. 244-256). Oxford: Oxford University Press.

53 **being lenient toward the past, actively appreciating the positive aspects of the current situation, and emphasizing possible future opportunities:** See p. 253 in Schneider, S.L. (2001). In search of realistic optimism: Meaning, knowledge, and warm fuzziness. *American Psychologist*, 56(3), 250-263.

54 **reframe this problem in the best possible light:** Carver, C.S., & Scheier, M.F. (2005). Optimism. In C.R. Snyder & S.J. Lopez (Eds.), *Handbook of Positive Psychology* (pp. 231-243). Oxford: Oxford University Press.

55 **Confidence, like optimism, is amenable to change.:** Maddux, J.E. (2005). Self-efficacy: The power of believing you can. In C.R. Snyder & S.J. Lopez (Eds.), *Handbook of Positive Psychology* (pp. 277-287). Oxford: Oxford University Press. Luthans, F., Youssef, C.M., & Avolio, B.J. (2007). *Psychological Capital: Developing the Human Competitive Edge*. Oxford: Oxford University Press.

55 **self-assurance primarily comes through mastery, observation, encouragement, and well-being:** Bandura, A. (2009). Cultivate self-efficacy for personal and organizational effectiveness. In E.A. Locke (Ed.), *Handbook of Principles of Organizational Behavior: Indispensible Knowledge for Evidence-Based Management*, 2nd ed. (pp 179-200). Hoboken, NJ: Wiley.

55 **"Our own attempts to control our environments …":** See p. 280 in Maddux, J. E. (2005). Self-efficacy: The power of believing you can. In C.R. Snyder & S.J. Lopez (Eds.), *Handbook of Positive Psychology* (pp. 277-287). Oxford: Oxford University Press.

56 **The more parallel a task is, the more likely it will boost our confidence.:** Luthans, F., Youssef, C.M., & Avolio, B.J. (2007). *Psychological Capital: Developing the Human Competitive Edge*. Oxford: Oxford University Press.

58 **How a leader frames these experiences helps determine their impact.:** Maddux, J.E. (2005). Self-efficacy: The power of believing you can. In C.R. Snyder & S.J. Lopez (Eds.), *Handbook of Positive Psychology* (pp. 277-287). Oxford: Oxford University Press.

62 **"What is good in my life right now?":** Fredrickson, B.L. (2009). Positivity: Groundbreaking Research Reveals How to Embrace the Hidden Strength of Positive Emotions, Overcome Negativity, and Thrive. New York: Crown Publisher.

Three: Meaning & Passion

67 *Everyone has his own specific vocation or mission in life*: Frankl, V.E. (2006). Man's Search for Meaning. Boston: Beacon Press.

67 *It's a Wonderful Life*: Capra, F. (Director). (1947). *It's a Wonderful Life*. Los Angeles: Liberty Films.

70 **"a calling is assumed to be unique to the person …":** See p. 46 in Wrzesniewski, A. (2012). Callings. In K.S. Cameron & G.M. Spreitzer (Eds.), *The Oxford Handbook of Positive Organizational Scholarship* (45-55). Oxford: Oxford University Press.

71 **spent 142 percent more time soliciting funds and raised 171 percent more revenue:** Grant, A.M., Campbell, E.M., Chen, G., Cottone, K., Lapedis, D., & Lee, K. (2007). Impact and the art of motivation maintenance: The effects of contact with beneficiaries on persistence behavior. *Organizational Behavior and Human Decision Processes*, 103, 53-67.

71 *... being human always points, and is directed, to something, or someone, other than oneself*: See pp. 110-111 in Frankl, V.E. (2006). *Man's Search for Meaning*. Boston: Beacon Press.

72 **lectured at 209 universities and was awarded 29 honorary doctorates:** *http://logotherapy.univie.ac.at/e/lifeandwork.html*.

72 **translated into 24 languages and had sold more than 10 million copies:** http://www.bookshopsantacruz.com/book/9780807014271.

72 **10 most influential books in America:** *http://www.nytimes.com/ 1991/11/20/books/booknotes-059091.html*.

72 **he submitted the paper, on Frankl's behalf:** Frankl, V.E. (1924). Zur mimischen bejahung und verneinung. *Internationale Zeitschriftfur Psychoanalyse*, 10, 437-438.

73 **"dirty Jewish swine."**: See p. 79 in Klingberg, H. (2001). *When Life Calls Out to Us: The Love and Lifework of Viktor and Elly Frankl*. New York: Random House.

73 **"an unconditional faith in life's unconditional meaning."**: See p. 83 in Klingberg, H. (2001). *When Life Calls Out to Us: The Love and Lifework of Viktor and Elly Frankl*. New York: Random House.

73 **"There is nothing in the world, ..."**: See pp. 103-104 in Frankl, V.E. (2006). *Man's Search for Meaning*. Boston: Beacon Press.

74 **"A man who becomes conscious of the responsibility he bears ..."**: See p. 79 in Frankl, V.E. (2006). *Man's Search for Meaning*. Boston: Beacon Press.

75 **Meaning is drawn from a cause to embrace:** Frankl, V.E. (2006). *Man's Search for Meaning*. Boston: Beacon Press.

75 **Meaning is a powerful stabilizing force:** Baumeister, R.F., & Vohs, K.D. (2005). The pursuit of meaningfulness in life. In C.R. Snyder & S.J. Lopez (Eds.)., *Handbook of Positive Psychology* (pp. 608-618). Oxford: Oxford University Press.

76 **givers do better than takers:** Grant, A. (2013). *Give and Take: A Revolutionary Approach to Success*. New York: Viking.

76 **"For success like happiness cannot be pursued ..."**: See pp. xiv-xv in Frankl, V.E. (2006). *Man's Search for Meaning*. Boston: Beacon Press.

76 **"an orientation to the welfare of others ..."**: See p. 34 in Peterson, C. (2006). *A Primer in Positive Psychology*. Oxford: Oxford University Press.

77 **an orientation to the welfare of others is more satisfying than an orientation to your own pleasure:** See pp. 34-36 in Peterson, C. (2006). *A Primer in Positive Psychology*. Oxford: Oxford University Press.

77 *Passion is what we are most deeply curious about* ...: See p. 69 in Levoy, G. (1997). *Calling: Finding and Following an Authentic Life*. New York: Three Rivers Press.

79 **our passions motivate us:** Loewenstein, G. (1994). The psychology of curiosity: A review and reinterpretation. *Psychological Bulletin*, 116(1), 75-98.

79 **your *best possible self***: King, L.A. (2001). The health benefits of writing about life goals. *Personality and Social Psychology Bulletin*, 27(7), 798-807. Sheldon, K.M., & Lyubomirsky, S. (2006). How to increase and sustain positive emotion: The effects of expressing gratitude and visualizing best possible selves. *The Journal of Positive Psychology*, 1(2), 73-82.

79 **"Imagine yourself in the future ...**: See p. 104 in Lyubomirsky, S. (2007). *The How of Happiness: A Scientific Approach to Getting the Life You Want*. New York: The Penguin Press.

80 **"How do you explain when things don't go as we assume ..."**: *http://www.youtube.com/watch?v=qp0HIF3SfI4*.

82 **Get your team members together and ask them ...:** These questions were adapted from a values survey developed by William Scott. See Scott, W.A. (1959). Empirical assessment of values and ideologies. *American Sociological Review*, 24(3), 299-309.

82 **humility and hunger:** The values "humility" and "hunger" are analogous to qualities that Jim Collins has identified in highly successful CEOs. According to Collins, the most effective executives exhibit a paradoxical blend of personal humility and professional will. These leaders are modest. They don't like to be in the spotlight and consistently give credit to others. At the same time, they have a fierce resolve and are relentless in their pursuit of excellence. He calls these leaders, Level-5 Leaders. See Collins, J. (2001). *Good to Great: Why Some Companies Make the Leap ... and Others Don't.* New York: HarperCollins.

83 **Meaning and passion develop in the context of our interactions with others.:** Wrzesniewski, A., Dutton, J.E., & Debebe, G. (2003). Interpersonal sensemaking and the meaning of work. *Research in Organizational Behavior*, 25, 93-135.

86 **a process of making a connection between what one is doing and why one is doing it:** Baumeister, R.F., & Vohs, K.D. (2005). The pursuit of meaningfulness in life. In C.R. Snyder & S.J. Lopez (Eds.), *Handbook of Positive Psychology* (pp. 608-618). Oxford: Oxford University Press.

86 **Even jobs that are considered by many to be menial or dirty can be imbued with meaning.:** Ashforth, B.E., & Kreiner, G.E. (1999). "How can you do it?": Dirty work and the challenge of constructing a positive identity. *The Academy of Management Review*, 24(3), 413-434. Pratt, M.G., & Ashford, B.E. (2003). Fostering meaningfulness in working at work. In K.S. Cameron, J.E. Dutton, & R.E. Quinn (Eds.), *Positive Organizational Scholarship* (309-327). San Francisco: Berrett-Koehler Publishers.

86 ***My job is equally important to the physician.*:** See pp. 71-72 in Cameron, K. (2008). Positive Leadership: Strategies for Extraordinary Performance. San Francisco: Berrett-Koehler Publishers.

88 ***"stop doing" lists*:** For more details regarding a "stop doing list" see Collins, J. (2001). *Good to Great: Why Some Companies Make the Leap ... and Others Don't.* New York: HarperCollins.

Four: Energy

93 *Energy—the sense of being eager to act and capable of action—is a critical, limited, but renewable resource*: Dutton, J.E. (2003). Energize Your Workplace: How to Create and Sustain High-Quality Connections at Work. San Francisco: Jossey-Bass.

93 **It's fundamentally related to creativity, grit, productivity, and well-being.:** Atwater, L., & Carmeli, A. (2009). Leader-member exchange, feelings of energy and involvement in creative work. *The Leadership Quarterly*, 20(3), 264-275. Kark, R., & Carmeli, A. (2009). Alive and creating: The mediating role of vitality and aliveness in the relationship between psychological safety and creative work involvement. *Journal of Organizational Behavior*, 30(6), 785-804. Cross, R., Baker, W., & Parker, A. (2003). What creates energy in organizations? *MIT Sloan Management Review*. 44(4), 51-56. Cole, M.S., Bruch, H., & Vogel, B. (2012). Energy at work: A measurement validation and linkage to unit effectiveness. *Journal of Organizational Behavior*, 33(4), 445-467.

93 **Employees who are energized by what they do are more committed and satisfied:** See p. 461 in Cole, M.S., Bruch, H., & Vogel, B. (2012). Energy at work: A measurement validation and linkage to unit effectiveness. *Journal of Organizational Behavior*, 33(4), 445-467.

93 **a greater impact on an organization:** Cross, R., Baker, W., & Parker, A. (2003). What creates energy in organizations? *MIT Sloan Management Review*, 44(4), 51-56.

94 **Energy is a complex, multifaceted phenomenon:** Cole, M.S., Bruch, H., & Vogel, B. (2012). Energy at work: A measurement validation and linkage to unit effectiveness. *Journal of Organizational Behavior*, 33(4), 445-467. Ryan, R.M., & Frederick, C. (1997). On energy, personality, and health: Subjective vitality as a dynamic reflection of well-being. *Journal of Personality*, 65(3), 529-565. Kaplan, S. (2001). Meditation, restoration, and the management of mental fatigue. *Environment and Behavior*, 33(4), 480-506.

95 **"The fullest representations of humanity show people to be curious, …":** See p. 68 in Ryan, R.M., & Deci, E.L. (2000). Self-determination theory and the facilitation of intrinsic motivation, social development, and well-being. *American Psychologist*, 55(1), 68-78.

96 **When we do things because we are good at them:** Ryan, R.M., & Deci, E.L. (2000). Facilitation of intrinsic motivation, social development, and well-being. *American Psychologist*, 55(1), 68-78. Reis, H.T., Sheldon, K.M., Gable, S.L., Roscoe, J., & Ryan, R.M. (2000). Daily well-being: The role of autonomy, competence, and relatedness. *Personality and Social Psychology Bulletin*, 26(4), 419-435. Nix, G.A., Ryan, R.M., Manly, J.B., & Deci, E.I. (1999). Revitalization through self-regulation: The effects of autonomous and controlled motivation on happiness and vitality. *Journal of Experimental Social Psychology*, 35(3), 266-284. Moller, A.C., Deci, E.L., & Ryan, R.M. (2006). Choice and ego-depletion: The moderating role of autonomy. *Personality and Social Psychology Bulletin*, 32(8), 1024-1036. Sheldon, K.M., Ryan, R., & Reis, H.T. (1996). What makes for a good day? Competence and autonomy in the day and in the person. *Personality and Social Psychology Bulletin*, 22(12), 1270-1279.

96 **We are invigorated by activities that we freely choose:** Ryan, R.M., Bernstein, J.H., & Brown, K.W. (2010). Weekends, work, and well-being: Psychological need satisfactions and day of the week effects on mood, vitality, and physical symptoms. *Journal of Social and Clinical Psychology*, 29(1), 95-122.

97 **three qualities of work relationships that contribute to vitality:** Dutton, J.E. (2006). *Energize Your Workplace: How to Create and Sustain High-Quality Connections at Work*. San Francisco: Jossey-Bass.

98 **Sometimes the best way to improve performance is to disengage:** Sonnentag and Fritz suggest four activities that help us to unwind and recuperate from work: (1) psychological detachment—not thinking about work, (2) relaxation experiences, (3) mastery experiences—skills/activities we have mastered, and (4) control over leisure time. See Sonnentag, S., & Fritz, C. (2007). The Recovery Experience Questionnaire: Development and validation of a measure for assessing recuperation and unwinding from work. *Journal of Occupational Health Psychology*, 12(3), 204-221.

98 **Individuals and teams that know when to step back are more creative and make better decisions.:** Dijksterhuis, A., Bos, M.W., Nordgren, L.F., & van Baaren, R.B. (2006). On making the right choice: The deliberation-without-attention effect. *Science*, 311(5763), 1005-1007. Rothbard, N.P., & Patil, S.V. (2012). Being there: Work engagement and positive organizational scholarship. In K.S. Cameron & G.M. Spreitzer (Eds.), *The Oxford Handbook of Positive Organizational Scholarship*, (pp. 56-69). Oxford: Oxford University Press.

98   **Even activities that require focus and attention can invigorate if they are pleasurable or interesting.:** Sonnentag, S., & Fritz, C. (2007). The Recovery Experience Questionnaire: Development and validation of a measure for assessing recuperation and unwinding from work. *Journal of Occupational Health Psychology*, 12(3), 204-221. Sonnentag, S., & Bayer, U.V. (2005). Switching off mentally: Predictors and consequences of psychological detachment from work during off-job time. *Journal of Occupational Health Psychology*, 10(4), 393-414.

98   **nature often has a natural revitalizing effect:** Kaplan, S. (1995). The restorative benefits of nature: Toward an integrative framework. *Journal of Environmental Psychology*, 15(3), 169-182.

98   **Physical activity increases energy and contributes to well-being.:** Thayer, R.E. (1987). Energy, tiredness, and tension effects of a sugar snack versus moderate exercise. *Journal of Personality and Social Psychology*, 52(1), 119-125. Thayer, R.E., Peters III, D.P., Takahashi, P.J., & Birkhead-Flight, A.M. (1993). Mood and behavior (smoking and sugar snacking) following moderate exercise: A partial test of self-regulation theory. *Personality and Individual Differences*, 14(1), 97-104.

98   **exercise lowers blood pressure and decreases the risk of heart disease:** PREMIER Collaborative Research Group. (2003). Effects of comprehensive lifestyle modification on blood pressure control. *The Journal of the American Medical Association*, 289(16), 2083-2093. Gaede, P., Vedel, P., Larsen, N., Jensen, G.V.H., Parving, H., & Pedersen, O. (2003). Multifactorial intervention and cardiovascular disease in patients with type 2 diabetes. *The New England Journal of Medicine*, 348(5), 383-393.

99   **Individuals who are active exhibit better mental processing speed and memory than their less active peers.:** Smith, P.J., Blumenthal, J.A., Hoffman, B.M., Cooper, H., Strauman, T.A., Welsh-Bohmer, K., Browndyke, J.N., & Sherwook, A. (2010). Aerobic exercise and neurocognitive performance: A meta-analytic review of randomized controlled trials. *Psychosomatic Medicine*, 72(3), 239-252.

99   **employees who are fit miss fewer days, are more satisfied with their jobs, and are more productive:** Aldana, S.G., & Pronk, N.P. (2001). Health promotion programs, modifiable health risks, and employee absenteeism. *Journal of Occupational and Environmental Medicine*, 43(1), 36-46. Tucker, L.A., Aldana, S.G., & Friedman, G.M. (*1990*) Cardiovascular fitness and absenteeism in 8,301 employed adults. *American Journal of Health Promotion*, 5(2), 140-145. Lechner, L., deVries, H., Adriaansen, S., & Drabbeis, L. (1997). Effects of an employee fitness program on reduced absenteeism. *Journal of Occupational and Environmental Medicine*, 39(9), 827-831. Bertera, R.L. (1991). The effects of behavioral risks on absenteeism and health-care costs in the workplace. *Journal of Occupational and Environmental Medicine*, 33(11), 1119-1124. Burton, W.N., Conti, D.J., Chen, C., Schultz, A.B., Alyssa, B., & Edington, D.W. (1999). The role of health risk factors and disease in worker productivity. *Journal of Occupational and Environmental Medicine*, 41(10), 863-877.

99   **the American College of Sports Medicine (ACSM) released exercise guidelines regarding the frequency, intensity, and duration of exercise in four areas:** Garber, C.E., Blissmer, B., Deschenes, M.R., Franklin, B.A., et al. (2011). Quantity and quality of exercise for developing and maintaining cardiorespiratory, musculoskeletal, and neuromotor fitness in apparently healthy adults: Guidance for prescribing exercise. *Medicine & Science in Sports & Exercise*, 43(7), 1334-1359.

100 **Proper nutrition and avoiding excess pounds reduce the risk of hypertension, diabetes, heart disease, and sleep disturbances.:**
http://www.nhlbi.nih.gov/guidelines/obesity/prctgd_c.pdf.

100 **miss more time at work, spend more on health care, and are less able to meet the physical demands of their job:** Robdard, H.W., Fox, K.M., & Grandy, S. (2009). Impact of obesity on work productivity and role disability in individuals with and at risk for diabetes mellitus. *American Journal of Health Promotion*, 23(5), 353-360. Pronk, N.P., Martinson, B., Kessler, R.C., Beck, A.L., Simon, G.E., & Wang, P. (2004). The association between work performance and physical activity, cardiorespiratory fitness, and obesity. *Journal of Occupational and Environmental Medicine*, 46(1), 19-25. Gates, D.M., Succop, P., Brehm, B.J., Gillespie, G.L., & Sommers, B.D. (2008). Obesity and presenteeism: The impact of body mass index on workplace productivity. *Journal of Occupational and Environmental Medicine*, 50(1), 39-45. Sullivan, P.W., Ghushchyan, V., and Ben-Joseph, R.H. (2008). The effect of obesity and cardiometabolic risk factors on expenditures and productivity in the United States. *Obesity*, 16(9), 2155-2162.

102 **Because they increase our risk for developing heart disease and diabetes, it's best to severely restrict their consumption.:**
http://www.heart.org/HEARTORG/GettingHealthy/FatsAndOils/Fats101/Trans-Fats_UCM_301120_Article.jsp.

102 **organizations like the Girl Scouts, McDonalds, and Wendy's have taken steps to reduce trans fats in the products they sell:** *http://www.girlscouts.org/news/news_releases/2006/gs_cookies_now_have_zero_trans_fats.asp*; http://www.nbcnews.com/id/16873869/#.UuZiv2Q_o62w.

102 **"Cutting back on all types of fat …":** See p. 81 in Willett, W. C. (2005). *Eat, Drink, and Be Healthy: The Harvard Medical School Guide To Healthy Eating.* New York, NY: Free Press.

103 **aren't getting the recommended amount of sleep:** Luckhaupt, S.E., Tak, S., & Calvert, G.M. (2010). The prevalence of short sleep duration by industry and occupation in the National Health Interview Survey. *Sleep*, 33(2), 149-159.

103 **Failure to get adequate rest is associated with an increased risk:** Gangwisch, J.E., Heymsfield, S.B., Boden-Albala, B, et al. (2006). Short sleep duration as a risk factor for hypertension: Analyses of the first National Health and Nutrition Examination Survey. *Hypertension,* 47(5), 833-839. Ayas, N.T., White, D.P., Manson, J.E., et al. (2003). A prospective study of sleep duration and coronary heart disease in women. *Archives of Internal Medicine*, 163(2), 205-209. Gangwisch, J.E., Heymsfield, S.B., Boden-Albala, B., et al. (2007). Sleep duration as a risk factor for diabetes incidence in a large U.S. sample. *Sleep*, 30(12), 1667-1673. Taheri, S., Lin, L., Austin, D., et al. (2004). Short sleep duration is associated with reduced leptin, elevated ghrelin, and increased body mass index. *PLOS Medicine*, 1(3), e62. Steptoe, A., Peacey, V., & Wardle, J. (2006) Sleep duration and health of young adults. *Archives of Internal Medicine*, 166(16), 1689-1692.

103 **an 18 percent increase in work-related incidents associated with human error on afternoon shifts and a 30 percent increase in such incidents on night shifts:** Burgess, P.A. (2007). Optimal shift duration and sequence: Recommended approach for short-term emergency response activations for public health and emergency management. *American Journal of Public Health*, 97(Suppl 1), S88-S92.

103 **tired workers accomplish less:** Rosekind, M.R., Gregory, K.B., Mallis, M.M., et al. (2010). The cost of poor sleep: Workplace productivity loss and associated costs. *Journal of Occupational and Environmental Medicine*, 52(1), 91-98.

104 **the current recommendation from the National Sleep Foundation is seven to nine hours per night:** http://www.sleepfoundation.org /article/how-sleep-works/how-much-sleep-do-we-really-need.

107 **Relationships based on respect, empowerment, and trust create enthusiasm.:** Dutton, J.E. (2003). *Energize Your Workplace: How to Create and Sustain High-Quality Connections at Work*. San Francisco: Jossey-Bass.

108 **provided better service and, interestingly, customers who interacted with them were more loyal to the hotel:** Salanova, M., Agut, S., & Peiro, J.M. (2005). Linking organizational resources and work engagement to employee performance and customer loyalty: The mediation of service climate. *Journal of Applied Psychology*, 90(6), 1217-1227.

Five: Undivided Attention

115 *"First of all," he said, ...*: See p. 48 in Lee, H. (1960). *To Kill a Mockingbird*. New York: HarperCollins Publishers.

115 **J.W. (Bill) Marriott, Jr. offers his perspective on the backstory behind the phenomenal success of Marriott International.:** Marriott, Jr., J.W., & Brown, K.A. (2013). *Without Reservations: How a Family Root Beer Stand Grew Into a Global Hotel Company*. San Diego: Luxury Custom Publishing, LLC.

116 **there is an innate need to connect:** Baumeister, R.F., & Leary, M. R. (1995). The need to belong: Desire for interpersonal attachments as a fundamental human motivation. *Psychological Bulletin*, 117(3), 497-529. Deci, E.L., & Ryan, R.M. (2008). Facilitating optimal motivation and psychological well-being across life's domains. *Canadian Psychology*, 49(1), 14-23.

116 **"... social relationships, or the relative lack thereof, constitute a major risk factor for health ...":** See p. 541 in House J.S., Landis K.R., & Umberson, D. (1988) Social relationships and health, *Science,* 241(4865), 540–545.

116 **"... individuals with adequate social relationships have a 50 percent greater likelihood of survival:** Holt-Lunstad, J., Smith, T.B., & Layton, J.B. (2010). Social relationships and mortality risk: A Meta-analytic review. *PLOS Medicine*, 7(7), e1000316.

117 **mutual respect and positive regard:** Rogers, C.R. (1961). *On Becoming a Person: A Therapist's View of Psychotherapy*. New York: Houghton Mifflin.

117 **Cohesive teams experience more positivity, attract better talent, and achieve more.:** Stephens, J.P., Heaphy, E., & Dutton, J.E. (2012). High-quality connections. In K.S. Cameron & G.M. Spreitzer (Eds.), *The Oxford Handbook of Positive Organizational Scholarship* (pp. 385-399). New York: Oxford University Press.

118 *collective intelligence*: Woolley, A.W., Chabris, C.F., Pentland, A., Hashmi, N., & Malone, T.W. (2010). Evidence for a collective intelligence factor in the performance of human groups. *Science*, 330(6004), 686-688.

118 **fight or flight:** Cannon, W. B. (1932). *The Wisdom of the Body*. New York, NY: W. W. Norton & Co., Inc.

118 **when a difficulty is prolonged it can harm our health:** Sapolsky, R. M. (2003). The physiology and pathophysiology of unhappiness. In D. Kahneman, E. Diener, & N. Schwarz (Eds.), *Well-Being: The Foundations of Hedonic Psychology* (pp. 453-469). New York, NY: Russell Sage Foundation.

119 **individuals with meaningful social ties are less physiologically responsive to the stress they encounter:** Heaphy, E.D., & Dutton, J.E. (2008). Positive social interactions and the human body at work: Linking organizations and physiology. *Academy of Management Review*, 33(1), 137-162.

119 **all too often there is a more sinister side to our social interactions:** Andersson, L.M., & Pearson, C.M. (1999). Tit for tat? The spiraling effect of incivility in the workplace, *Academy of Management Review*, 24(3), 452-471.

119 **stopped doing their best:** Pearson, C.M., Andersson, L.M., & Porath, C.L. (2000). Assessing and attacking workplace incivility. *Organizational Dynamics*, 29(2), 123-137.

119 **Little, if anything, causes disengagement and kills momentum like interpersonal strife.:** Spreitzer, G., & Porath, C. (2012). Creating sustainable performance: If you give your employees the chance to learn and grow, they'll thrive—and so will your organization. *Harvard Business Review*. 90(1/2), 92-99. Pearson, C.M., & Porath, C.L. (2005). On the nature, consequences, and remedies of workplace incivility: No time for "nice"? Think again. *Academy of Management Executive*, 19(1), 7-18.

119 **characteristic ways of interacting:** Stephens, J.P., Heaphy, E., & Dutton, J.E. (2012). High-quality connections. In K.S. Cameron, & G.M. Spreitzer (Eds.), *The Oxford Handbook of Positive Organizational Scholarship* (pp. 385-399). Oxford: Oxford University Press.

120 **personnel who feel valued provide better customer service:** *http://businessjournal.gallup.com/content/23893/can-employees-friends-boss.aspx*.

120 **"… doing a kindness …":** See p. 20 in Seligman, M.E.P. (2011). *Flourish: A Visionary New Understanding of Happiness and Well-Being.* New York: Free Press.

120 **Individuals who offer support to friends and family live longer than their contemporaries:** Brown, S.L., Nesse, R.M., Vinokur, A.D., & Smith D.M. (2003). Providing social support may be more beneficial than receiving it: Results from a prospective study of mortality, *Psychological Science*, 14(4), 320-327.

120 **"An essential part of true listening is the discipline of bracketing, …":** See p. 127 in Peck, M. S. (1978). *The Road Less Traveled: A New Psychology of Love, Traditional Values and Spiritual Growth*. New York, NY: Simon and Schuster.

121 **meaningful conversations and feeling understood and appreciated make the most consistent contribution to our sense of closeness with others:** Reis, H.T., Sheldon, K.M., Gable, S.L., Roscoe, J., & Ryan, R.M. (2000). Daily well-being: The role of autonomy, competence, and relatedness. *Personality and Social Psychology Bulletin*, 26(4), 419-435.

122 **"Qualitative observations of the teams showed that high-performance teams …":** See p. 749 in Losada, M., & Heaphy, E. (2004). The role of positivity and connectivity in the performance of business teams: A nonlinear dynamics model. *American Behavioral Scientist*, 47(6), 740-765.

122 **the number-one reason people leave their job is they don't feel appreciated:** See pp. 15-17 in Rath, T., & Clifton, D.O. (2009). *How Full Is Your Bucket? (Expanded Anniversary Edition).* New York: Gallup Press.

124 **The impact of a positive experience is augmented and extended when it's shared.:** Langston, C. A. (1994). Capitalizing on and coping with daily-life events: Expressive responses to positive events. *Journal of Personality and Social Psychology*, 67 (6), 1112-1125.

124 **By listening carefully, asking questions, and taking interest in what is revealed,:** Gable, S.L., Reis, H.T., Impett, E.A., & Asher, E.R. (2004). What do you do when things go right? Interpersonal benefits of sharing positive events. *Journal of Personality and Social Psychology*, 87(2), 228-245.

124 **develops either a basic trust in others and the environment or, unfortunately, a basic mistrust:** Erikson, E.H. (1950). *Childhood and Society*. New York: W.W. Norton & Co.

125 **People build trust by acting in a trustworthy manner.:** Mishra, A.K., & Mishra, K.E. (2012). Positive organizational scholarship and trust in leaders. In K.S. Cameron & G.M. Spreitzer (Eds.), *The Oxford Handbook of Positive Organizational Scholarship* (pp. 449-461). Oxford: Oxford University Press.

125 **trust is a way of acting toward others:** Dutton, J.E. (2003). *Energizing the Workplace: How to Create and Sustain High-Quality Connections at Work*. San Francisco, Jossey-Bass. Mishra, A.K., & Mishra, K.E. (2012). Positive organizational scholarship and trust in leaders. In K.S. Cameron & G.M. Spreitzer (Eds.), *The Oxford Handbook of Positive Organizational Scholarship* (pp. 449-461). Oxford: Oxford University Press.

126 **Perspective taking is the "capacity to consider the world from another individual's viewpoint.":** Galinsky, A.D., Maddux, W.W., Gilin, D., & White, J.B. (2008). Why it pays to get inside the head of your opponent: The differential effects of perspective taking and empathy in negotiations. *Psychological Science*, 19(4), 378-384.

128 **"The results revealed that intimates in satisfying marriages perceive more virtue in their partners ...":** See p. 600 in Murray, S.L., Holmes, J.G., Dolderman, D., & Griffin, D.W. (2000). What the motivated mind sees: Comparing friends' perspectives to married partners' views of each other. *Journal of Experimental Social Psychology*, 36(6), 600-620.

128 **idealism is associated with more beneficial outcomes than realism:** Murray, S.L., Holmes, J.G., & Griffin, D.W. (1996). The benefits of positive illusions: Idealization and the construction of satisfaction in close relationships. *Journal of Personality and Social Psychology*, 70(1), 79-98.

128 **Self-fulfilling prophecy:** Murray, S.L., Holmes, J.G., & Griffin, D.W. (1996). The self-fulfilling nature of positive illusions in romantic relationships: Love is not blind, but prescient. *Journal of Personality and Social Psychology*, 71(6), 1155-1180.

128 **Positive perceptions of others lead to stronger bonds, less conflict, and greater satisfaction.:** Murray, S.L., & Holmes, J.G. (1997). A leap of faith? Positive illusions in romantic relationships. *Personality and Social Psychology Bulletin*, 23(6), 586-604.

129 **one of the most effective ways a leader can inspire a team is to enable progress:** Dutton, J.E. (2003). *Energizing the Workplace: How to Create and Sustain High-Quality Connections at Work*. San Francisco, Jossey-Bass.

130 **A popular view of goal setting suggests that moderately difficult challenges are the most motivating.:** Atkinson, J.W. (1958). Toward experimental analysis of human motivation in terms of motives, expectancies, and incentives. In J.W. Atkinson (Ed.), *Motives in Fantasy, Actions and Society* (pp. 288-305). Princeton, NJ: Van Nostrand.

130 **difficult tasks generate the greatest effort and lead to the highest level of achievement:** Locke, E.A. (2005). Setting goals for life and happiness. In C.R. Snyder & S.J. Lopez (Eds.), *Handbook of Positive Psychology* (pp. 299-312). Oxford: Oxford University Press.

Six: Positivity

137 **Happy employees produce more than unhappy ones:** Spreitzer, G., & Porath, C. (2012). Creating sustainable performance: If you give your employees the chance to learn and grow, they'll thrive—and so will your organization. *Harvard Business Review*, 90(1/2), 92-99.

138 **The transfer of emotion was automatic and immediate.:** Dimberg, U., & Thunberg, M. (1998). Rapid facial reactions to emotional facial expressions. *Scandinavian Journal of Psychology*, 39(1), 39-45. Dimberg, U., Thunberg, M., & Elmehed, K. (2000). Unconscious facial reactions to emotional facial expressions. *Psychological Science*, 11(1), 86-89.

138 **National Heart Institute:** The National Heart Institute is currently known as the National Heart, Lung, and Blood Institute (NHLBI).

138 **Framingham Heart Study:** Additional information regarding the Framingham Heart Study is available at http://www.framinghamheartstudy.org/.

138 **the closer we are geographically to another individual, the more likely we will be influenced by his or her mood:** Fowler, J.H., & Christakis, N.A. (2008). Dynamic spread of happiness in a large social network: Longitudinal analysis over 20 years in the Framingham Heart Study. *British Medical Journal*, 337, a2338.

138 **Emotions are not only contagious in communities like the one studied in the Framingham Heart Study, but also in our homes and in organizations of all kinds.:** Bono, J.E., & Ilies, R., (2006). Charisma, positive emotions, and mood contagion. *The Leadership Quarterly*, 17(4), 317-334. Sy, T., Cote, S., & Saavedra, R. (2005). The contagious leader: Impact of the leader's mood on the mood of group members, group affective tone, and group processes. *Journal of Applied Psychology*, 90(2), 295-305.

138 **an organization's emotional climate is influenced from the top:** Anderson, C., & Thompson, L.L. (2004). Affect from the top down: How powerful individuals' positive affect shapes negotiations. *Organizational Behavior and Human Decision Process*, 95, 125-139.

139 **receive more favorable evaluations:** Cropanzano, R., & Wright, T.A. (1999). A 5-year study of change in the relationship between well-being and job performance. *Consulting Psychology Journal: Practice and Research*, 51(4), 252-265.

139 **are persistent when attempting difficult tasks:** Miles, D.E., Borman, W.E., Spector, P.E., & Fox, S. (2002). Building an integrative model of extra role work behaviors: A comparison of counterproductive work behavior with organizational citizenship behavior. *International Journal of Selection and Assessment*, 10(1/2), 51-57.

139 **experience greater satisfaction at work:** Weiss, H.M., Nicholas, J.P., & Daus, C.S. (1999). An examination of the joint effects of affective experiences and job beliefs on job satisfaction and variations in affective experiences over time. *Organizational Behavior and Human Decision Processes*, 78(1), 1-24.

139 **make more money:** Deluga, R.J., & Masson, S. (2000). Relationship of resident assistance conscientiousness, extraversion, and positive affect with rated performance. *Journal of Research in Personality*, 34(2), 225-235. Graham, C., Eggers, A., & Sukhtankar, S. (2004). Does happiness pay? An exploration based on panel data from Russia. *Journal of Economic Behavior & Organization*, 55, 319-342. Staw, B.M., Sutton, R.I., & Pelled, L.H. (1994). Employee positive emotion and favorable outcomes at the workplace. *Organizational Science*, 5(1), 51-71. Diener, E., Nickerson, C., Lucas, R.E., & Sandvik, E. (2002). Dispositional affect and job outcomes. *Social Indicators Research*, 59, 229-259.

139 **positive feelings have a significant impact on individual health and well-being:** An extensive review of the literature examining the connection between emotions and health and well-being is found in Lyubomirsky, S., King, L., & Diener, E. (2005). The benefits of frequent positive affect: Does happiness lead to success? *Psychological Bulletin*, 131(6), 803-855.

139 **have more meaningful and satisfying relationships:** Diener, E., & Seligman, M.E.P. (2002). Very happy people. *Psychological Science*, 13(1), 81-84.

139 **report less depression:** Fredrickson, B.L., Tugade, M.M., Waugh, C.E., & Larkin, G.R. (2003). What good are positive emotions in crisis?: A prospective study of resilience and emotions following the terrorist attacks on the United States on September 11th, 2001. *Journal of Personality and Social Psychology*, 84(2), 365-376.

140 **Positivity even offers protection from the common cold.:** Cohen, S., Doyle, W.J., Turner, R.B., Alper, C.M., & Skoner, D.P. (2003) Emotional style and susceptibility to the common cold. *Psychosomatic Medicine*, 65(4), 652-657.

140 **a full smile:** A full smile is also called a Duchenne smile. This is a smile involving the entire face. The corners of the lips are raised and the muscles are contracted around the eyes elevating the cheeks.

140 **lived an average of seven years longer:** Abel, E.L., & Kruger, M.L. (2010). Smile intensity in photographs predicts longevity. *Psychological Science*, 21(4), 542-544.

140 **young women who were more positive, as indicated by their smiles:** Harker, L., & Keltner, D. (2001). Expression of positive emotion in women's college yearbook pictures and their relationship to personality and life outcomes across adulthood. *Journal of Personality and Social Psychology*, 80(1), 112-124.

140 **individuals who had written statements high in positive content lived up to ten years longer:** Danner, D.D., Snowdon, D.A., & Friesen, W.V. (2001). Positive emotions in early life and longevity: Findings from the nun study. *Journal of Personality and Social Psychology*, 80(5), 804-813.

141 **positivity elicits a very different response, motivating us to *broaden* our understanding and *build* on our experience:** Fredrickson, B.L. (2009). *Positivity: Groundbreaking Research Reveals How to Embrace the Hidden Strength of Positive Emotions, Overcome Negativity, and Thrive*. New York: Crown Publishing Group.

141 **Positive emotions help us adapt to and recover more quickly from negative experiences.:** Fredrickson, B.L., & Levenson, R.W. (1998). Positive emotions speed recovery from the cardiovascular sequelae of negative emotions. *Cognition and Emotion*, 12(2), 191-220.

141 **a significant contribution to our intellectual, physical, social, and psychological resources:** Fredrickson, B. (2003). The value of positive emotions: The emerging science of positive psychology is coming to understand why it's good to feel good. *American Scientist*, 91(4), 330-335.

142 **creating an upward spiral, which promotes health and well-being, as well as greater productivity and success:** Fredrickson, B.L., & Joiner, T. (2002). Positive emotions trigger upward spirals toward emotional well-being. *Psychological Science*, 13(2), 172-175.

142 **bad is stronger than good:** Baumeister, R.F., Bratslavsky, E., Finkenauer, C., & Vohs, K.D. (2001). Bad is stronger than good. *Review of General Psychology*, 5(4), 323-370.

143 **we rapidly adapt to the good things that happen:** Kahneman, D., Krueger, A.B., Schkade, D., Schwarz, N., & Stone, A.A. (2006). Would you be happier if you were rich? A focusing illusion. *Science*, 312(5782), 1908-1910. Frederick, S., & Lowenstein, G. (1999). Hedonic adaptation. In Kahneman, D., Diener, E., & Schwartz, N. (eds.), *Well-Being: The Foundations of Hedonic Psychology* (pp. 302-329). New York: Russell Sage.

143 **individuals who have won the lottery adjust quickly to their newfound wealth:** Brickman, P., Coates, D., & Janoff-Bulman, R. (1978). Lottery winners and accident victims: Is happiness relative? *Journal of Personality and Social Psychology*, 36(8), 917-927.

144 **We are not good forecasters of how we will be affected by a particular event.:** Wilson, T.D., & Gilbert, D.T. (2005). Affective forecasting: Knowing what to want. *Current Directions in Psychological Science*, 14(3), 131-134.

144 ***3 to 1*:** Fredrickson, B.L. (2009). Positivity: Groundbreaking Research Reveals How to Embrace the Hidden Strength of Positive Emotions, Overcome Negativity, and Thrive. New York: Crown Publishers.

144 ***5 to 1*:** Gottman, J.M. (1994). What Predicts Divorce? The Relationship Between Marital Processes and Marital Outcomes. Hillsdale, New Jersey: Lawrence Erlbaum Associates.

145 ***6 to 1*:** Losada, M., & Heaphy, E. (2004). The role of positivity and connectivity in the performance of business teams: A nonlinear dynamics model. *American Behavioral Scientist*, 47(6), 740-765.

145 **Is it possible to be *too* positive?:** For a discussion of the possibility that too much positivity could be harmful, see pp. 135-137 in Fredrickson, B.L. (2009). *Positivity: Groundbreaking Research Reveals How to Embrace the Hidden Strength of Positive Emotions, Overcome Negativity, and Thrive*. New York: Crown Publishers.

146 **mentally review what occurred in your life:** Kahneman, D., Krueger, A.B., Schkade, D.A., Schwarz, N., & Stone, A.A. (2004). A survey method for characterizing daily life experience: The Day Reconstruction Method. *Science*, 306 (5702), 1776-1780.

147 **activities others have found useful in their pursuit of happiness:** This list of activities associated with positivity is adapted from Fredrickson, B.L. (2009) *Positivity: Groundbreaking Research Reveals How to Embrace the Hidden Strength of Positive Emotions, Overcome Negativity, and Thrive*. New York: Crown Publishers. and Lyubomirsky, S. (2007). *The How of Happiness: A Scientific Approach to Getting the Life You Want*. New York: The Penguin Press.

148 **one of the best ways to extend and augment the positivity we feel is to tell others about our blessings:** Langston, C.A. (1994). Capitalizing on and coping with daily-life events: Expressive responses to positive events. *Journal of Personality and Social Psychology*, 67(6), 1112-1125.

148 **tell them about your successes:** Gable, S.L., Reis, H.T., Impett, E.A., & Asher, E.R. What do you do when things go right? The intrapersonal and interpersonal benefits of sharing positive events. *Journal of Personality and Social Psychology*, 87(2), 228-245.

148 **"… if there's any 'secret' to becoming happier …":** See p. 70 in Lyubomirsky, S. (2007). *The How of Happiness: A Scientific Approach to Getting the Life You Want*. New York: The Penguin Press.

148 **As a leader, you set the tone.:** Bono, J.E., & Ilies, R. (2006). Charisma, positive emotions and mood contagion. *The Leadership Quarterly*, 17(4), 317-334.

149 **"When we compared our study participants' best days …":** See p. 81 in Amabile, T.M., & Kramer, S.J. (2007). Inner work life: Understanding the subtext of business performance. *Harvard Business Review*, 85(5), 72-83.

149 **There are a number of specific actions leaders can take to ensure those they lead experience success.:** Amabile, T.M., & Kramer, S.J. (2007). Inner work life. *Harvard Business Review*. May 2007, 72-83.

150 **your energy and your practices rub off:** Bono, J.E., & Ilies, R. (2006). Charisma, positive emotions and mood contagion. *The Leadership Quarterly*, 17(4), 317-344. Anderson, C., & Thompson, L. (2004). Affect from the top down: How powerful individuals' positive affect shapes negotiations. *Organizational Behavior and Human Decision Processes*, 95, 125-139.

Conclusion: Habit

157 **We Are What We Repeatedly Do:** See p. 61 in Durant, W. (1926). The Story of Philosophy: The Lives and Opinions of the World's Greatest Philosophers from Plato to John Dewey. New York: Simon & Schuster, Inc.
157 **Jim Ryun:** Jim Ryun is a former world record holder in the mile run.
158 **rewind your life, as if it were a video recording, and pause in order to recall specific situations:** Kahneman, D., Krueger, A.B., Schkade, D.A., Schwarz, N., & Stone, A.A. (2004). A survey method for characterizing daily life experience: The Day Reconstruction Method. *Science*, 306 (5702), 1776-1780.

About the Author

Gene Harker is an award-winning teacher at a large medical school in the Midwest. The recipient of four advanced degrees, Dr. Harker has more than 25 years of experience as a physician, psychologist, and professor. He is an author and frequent seminar speaker whose passion is helping individuals and organizations thrive. He lives in Indianapolis with his wife Lynette. They have two married children and a grandchild.

Printed in Great Britain
by Amazon.co.uk, Ltd.,
Marston Gate.